# FRONTIER VISION

IN 1987, A SMALL GROUP OF ENTERPRISING CANADIANS RECLAIMED THE HERITAGE OF THE HUDSON'S BAY COMPANY'S NORTHERN STORES DIVISION. THEY REACHED BACK IN TIME TO NAME THE NEW ENTITY "THE NORTH WEST COMPANY" AND IT GREW INTO A TRUE SUCCESS STORY. THIS BOOK TELLS THAT STORY AND IS DEDICATED TO THE PEOPLE OF THE NORTH WEST COMPANY AND THE COMMUNITIES THAT WE SERVE.

Edward Kennedy
*President and CEO, The North West Company*

**Library and Archives Canada Cataloguing in Publication**

MacDonald, Jake, 1949-
    Frontier vision : the rebirth of the North West Company / Jake MacDonald ; prologue by Charles Foran.

Includes index.
ISBN 978-0-9866361-5-8

    1. North West Company—History—20th century. 2. North West Company—History—21st century. I. Title. II. Title: Rebirth of the North West Company.

HF5469.23.C24N67 2013    381'.456413097    C2013-901944-8

Printed in China

CREATIVE DIRECTOR John Wellwood
WRITERS Jake MacDonald, Charles Foran
DESIGNER Cathy Smith
PHOTO EDITORS Natasha Lakos, Megan Lau
PRODUCTION COORDINATOR Kate Moore
INDEXER Iva Cheung
COPYEDITOR Renate Preuss
PROOFREADER Marial Shea

THE REBIRTH OF THE NORTH WEST COMPANY

# FRONTIER VISION

BY JAKE MacDONALD
PROLOGUE BY CHARLES FORAN

# CONTENTS

"CONTINENTAL" COCKED HAT. (1776)

"NAVY" COCKED HAT. (1800)

ARMY. (1837)

CLERICAL. (Eighteenth Century)

(THE WELLINGTON.) (1812)

CIVIL.

(THE PARIS BEAU.) (1815)

"NONSUCH" for THE HUDSON'S BAY COMPANY. GENERAL ARRANGEMENT

SCALE ½ INCH = 1 FOOT.

DRAWING Nº 931.

DRAWN BY Peter M. Wood RSMA.

Rodney Warington Smyth, AMRINA. Falmouth, Cornwall, England.

## PROLOGUE
# BOLD MEN, BIG DREAMS, WILD COUNTRY:
## THE NORTHWEST COMPANY, 1668–1988

### THE NONSUCH

From the start, it was the business of adventure as much as the adventure of business. On September 29, 1668, the British ship the *Nonsuch* landed at the southern end of James Bay. It wasn't a moment too soon for what was, in fact, an expedition to establish trade in the shortly to be decreed territory of Rupert's Land. Crew members raced to build a crude fort before the notorious new world winter set in. When the resident Cree showed up in the spring to trade furs, and the *Nonsuch* managed the long trip back to England with the lucrative cargo in its hold, a formidable, and challenging, business was born. So, it turned out, was a great adventure in surviving and thriving in that new world and with those native residents — at least, for the more intrepid and entrepreneurial of frontier merchants.

Rupert's Land was a preposterous 1670 "gift" from King Charles to his cousin Prince Rupert and the 17 other charter members of the Hudson's Bay Company. It wasn't only that the English monarch believed any land not directly ruled by a "Christian prince" was his to freely grant. The size of the Royal Charter, too, was outlandish. By including all land in the Hudson Bay watershed, Charles signed over to a handful of insiders a land mass that today includes much of Northern Ontario and Quebec, all of Manitoba and most of Saskatchewan and southern Alberta, along with a good portion of Nunavut.

All told, some 3.9 million square kilometers, or 40 percent of modern-day Canada, decreed a territorial monopoly for a period of two hundred years. A great deal, for some.

The HBC made limited, or perhaps cautious, use of the gift. Europeans loved their beaver-felt hats, especially fashion-minded men. So popular were beaver top and Wellington hats, army and navy hats, "Continental" cocked hats and the Paris Beau, that for a period the headdresses of men were simply known as "Beavers." The market was vigorous, and the animals harvested, via trading with indigenous people in Rupert's Land, were superb. The company soon had trading posts ringing Hudson's Bay. After an early commercial bump — due to pesky French traders who operated along the fringes of their monopoly and attacked and occupied several forts — the HBC enjoyed decades of lucrative trading.

Based in London, with an established seasonal commercial plan of having natives bring the pelts to their posts for transport across the Atlantic, the HBC saw little reason to interact with the landscape, or the people, of "its" territory. It certainly showed modest cultural or human interest in either, and little impulse to explore what lay beyond the generous charter. Other traders, however, forced by the HBC monopoly to venture deeper into the continent, were more engaged.

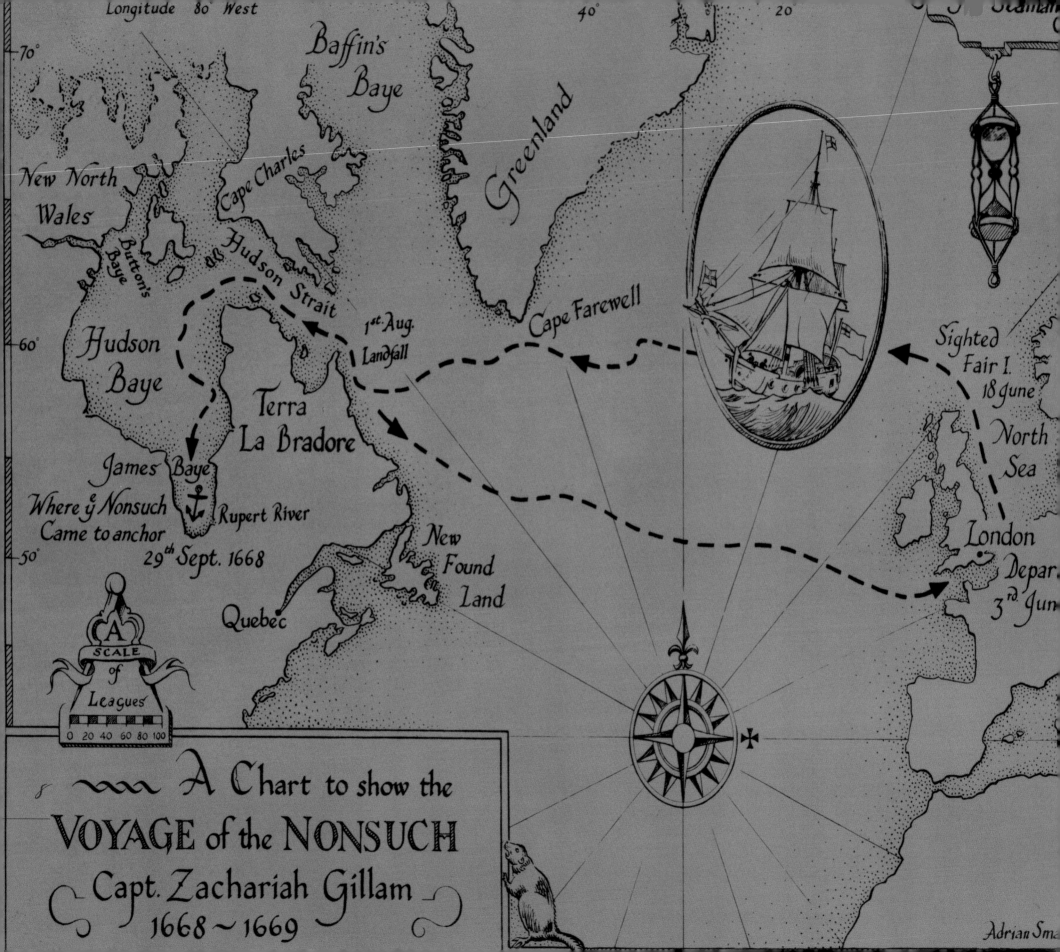

Longitude 80 West          40°          20°

70°

Baffin's Baye

New North Wales

Cape Charles

Greenland

Button's Baye

Hudson Strait

60°          Hudson Baye

1st Aug. Landfall

Cape Farewell

Sighted Fair I. 18 June

North Sea

Terra La Bradore

James Baye

Where ye Nonsuch Came to anchor 29th Sept. 1668

Rupert River

London

Depar. 3rd Jun

50°

SCALE of Leagues
0  20 40 60 80 100

New Found Land

Quebec

A Chart to show the
VOYAGE of the NONSUCH
Capt. Zachariah Gillam
1668 ~ 1669

Adrian Sm

FUR TRADE

FUR TRADE

OPPOSITE: BECAUSE OF ITS SMALL SIZE, THE NONSUCH COULD BE SAILED UP-RIVER AND TAKEN OUT OF WATER SO THE THICK ICE OF JAMES BAY WOULDN'T CRUSH HER. PREVIOUS (FROM LEFT): EXPLORER SIMON FRASER LED A CREW OF 18 VOYAGEURS AND TWO CARRIER NATIVE GUIDES DOWN THE "PIONEER HIGHWAY"; VARIATIONS ON A 16TH-CENTURY FASHION TREND, THE BEAVER HAT.

THE NONSUCH DROPPED ANCHOR AT THE SOUTHERN END OF JAMES BAY. WASKAGANISH ON JAMES BAY WAS NORTH AMERICA'S FIRST TRADING POST.

French, American and Scots entrepreneurs travelled along traditional waterways and wintered on the shores of frozen rivers and lakes. In warm weather they used lightweight canoes; during the long winter months, snowshoes and toboggans were the means of transport. These men ate local foods and took local medicine when sick. They formed alliances and friendships with native and Metis traders and trappers, who shared with them life-saving information about how to get by in the daunting environment. Some of these traders fell for native women, making homes and raising families.

In short, these were 18th-century Europeans of a different sort. For them, Canada was not a colonial outpost to be suffered for a period. Instead, it was where they lived and, most likely, would die. The considerable hardships were matched by the beauty and challenge of the land; the ongoing risks were offset by the prospect of great reward, or at least lives of self-sufficiency and independence. Having been expelled by the English during the Highland clearances of the 1740s, for instance, exiled Scotsmen began writing from Montreal to tell family and friends of opportunity that awaited them across the ocean. These early honorary Nor'westers couldn't always avoid the reach of global politics — French traders had to swallow the official withdrawal of France in 1763, folding New France into the British Empire — but for the most part they could operate below the radar of those distant European wars.

A more regional conflict permanently changed not only the trade but Canada itself. When the British, then fighting the American rebels in the Thirteen Colonies, placed an embargo on private shipping in the Great Lakes, the governor of Quebec decided to stop issuing licenses for trading furs. Supplies failed to reach traders, called *hivernants*, wintering in the west; in Montreal, many merchants were ruined. Only a coalition of free traders was likely to persuade the governor to rethink his position. By 1779, the business partnership had a name, the Northwest Company (a coat of arms showing a beaver below a tree and the apt motto of "Perseverance") and assurances that the licenses would be issued again. The behemoth HBC, snug in its Royal Charter, had a new rival to contend with. The upstart company wasn't nearly its size, but was already its superior in ingenuity and resourcefulness.

## FREE TRADERS, FEARLESS EXPLORERS

Two Nor'westers of distinct temperaments typified the company's identity in its early days. Their stories, and their fates, couldn't be more different. One of the nine original partners, McBeath and Co., employed a darkly charismatic American named Peter Pond. In spring 1778, Pond, a veteran soldier and independent trader who probably found his way to the Canadian northwest after killing a man in a duel, was leading a five-canoe expedition from the mouth of the Sturgeon River, near Prince Albert, Saskatchewan, up into uncharted Athabasca territories. As much explorer as trader, Pond drove his crew a thousand miles north to near Lake Athabasca.

No less remarkably, the men wintered there in a cabin, trading with the Chipewyan to survive. The following spring they returned with 140 packs of excellent dark pelts for the warehouse in Montreal.

Pond's excursion expanded the potential territory for traders with the stamina to press further north and west of Rupert's Land. The Europeans still did not know how much more rugged, mountainous continent laid in either of those directions, lending their growing enterprise a romantic, even heroic, quality. Small groups set out each spring to push the boundaries of the known (to them, at least) in modest canoes, aware that they could not possibly retrace their steps before the early snows. Such daunting circumstances demanded men who were at once fierce and fueled as much by dreams as commerce.

Peter Pond was probably not a gentleman — evidence linked him to two further murders of trading rivals — but he had guts, and vision, aplenty. During his final winter in Athabasca, Pond passed the time working on a map depicting what he believed was the still elusive Northwest Passage connecting Europe to Asia. The map, though wildly inaccurate, was still more forward looking than its cartographer, who wound up dying in obscurity and poverty.

Overseeing those Montreal warehouses, in contrast, was a man now widely credited as being Canada's first business mogul. Simon McTavish headed up McTavish & Co., another of the small traders who banded together to compete with the HBC. This son of a Scottish soldier had immigrated to America at the age of 13, apprenticing in a fur

warehouse and shortly gaining a reputation for enjoying "good wine, good oysters, and pretty girls." By 1790, he was both a senior partner in the Northwest Company, holding a controlling interest, and its *de facto* Chief Director. Building a unified and successful commercial empire out of no fewer than four different co-partnerships over two decades took someone who was at the same time a conciliator and a mastermind. The handsome, imperious McTavish, dubbed "Le Marquis" for his grand personal lifestyle, was both.

He was also a tough boss for a tough business. Known for his tenacity and temper equally — he, too, had fought duels, and once deliberately shot wide of a man who had challenged him over a silly slight — and not above allowing employees to use physical intimidation with rivals, McTavish was equally generous and loyal. He found work for dozens of extended family members, all presumed Scotsman of the "hardy, courageous, shrewd and proud" kind. (The company was rife with Mackenzies, McGillivrays, McLeods, Findleys, Frasers and Camerons, many of them related. Alongside such an abundance of Macdonalds that they had to be further identified by their highland addresses, the partnership resembled from the outset an ongoing clan reunion across the Atlantic.) If fur trading was simple in theory — the acquiring, storing, shipping and selling of furs for European markets — it was complex in fact. It also took its slow 18th-century time: a two-to-three-year cycle to see any return on working capital was not uncommon on a shipment, with the risk of losing the investment to accident always a

factor. Though McTavish traveled to England several winters in succession to plead with the prime minister to cancel the Royal Charter, and likewise tried negotiating with HBC to use their Hudson Bay water route, he concentrated on how to make the best of a bad situation. Out of adversity came innovation and patient commerce.

The HBC monopoly obliged the Northwest Company to take the longer, more treacherous routes in and out of the heart of the continent. The HBC had some 1,500 fewer canoe-miles to travel with their stock, a huge time and money savings. To make up, Nor'westers moved swiftly and skillfully, adapting to the landscape. Canoes had long been essential to the fur trade. HBC's heavy York boats may have worked fine in bays and lakes, but river travel, nearly always involving portages, required a lighter vessel. Nor'westers employed their own large freight canoes, called Montreal canoes, or *canot du maitre*, crewed by 10 men and able to carry four tons of freight. But they relied as much on the smaller *canot du nord*. This craft was an extraordinary engineering feat, custom designed for the Canadian Shield, while still holding two tons and six paddlers. It could be carried across portages, some as long as 10 miles, by just two powerful and tireless men.

Equally revolutionary to the company's success was a simple foodstuff. To feed a crew of 6, or 10, over the months of 12-hour paddling days needed to travel from the Lachine Rapids outside Montreal to Lake Winnipeg required either frequent stops to hunt, or the *voyageur* equivalent of army C-rations. By bartering pemmican, natives and

1783
THE NORTH WEST
COMPANY TOOK OVER OLD
FRENCH TRADING POST AT
SAVLT STE MARIE

S.S.M.H.S

> "Voyageurs may have craved the odd buffalo tongue or boiled fetal calf as gastronomic relief, but most days they paddled solely on pemmican — up to two pounds of it, chewed without complaint."

Metis provided canoe crews with their essential fuel. Pulverize dried buffalo meat, mix it with melted animal tallow and Saskatoon berries, and then fill a rawhide bag with the substance, and you had pemmican. It wasn't especially tasty, but it was lightweight, long-lasting, nutritious (the berries provided vitamin C), and could be eaten raw, while still maintaining the optimum 40-strokes-per-minute paddle speed. Voyageurs may have craved the odd buffalo tongue or boiled fetal calf as gastronomic relief, but most days they paddled solely on pemmican — up to two pounds of it, chewed without complaint. Not that complaining would have done them any good; starvation, frostbite, death by illness or accident kept stark company with these hearty, and legendary, river rats.

Like the adoption of canoe travel, pemmican symbolized the company's recognition that it had to be alert and responsive to the impossibly large, difficult and mostly uncharted territory where it wished to conduct business. Just as natives depended on the goods — mostly blankets and linen, cutlery and kettles, handkerchiefs and shoes, along with smaller quantities of weapons and alcohol — it traded for its animal furs, Nor'westers were dependent on natives not only for the pelts themselves, but as guides and translators, advisors and, occasionally, friends. From a contemporary point of view, this mutual dependency and willingness to integrate with the frontier in virtually every respect is an obvious way to conduct affairs. But as the methods of the HBC demonstrated, colonial businessmen, especially Europeans with a strong sense of racial superiority, were frequently oblivious to local conditions, insisting on doing things as they did them back in England or Germany or France. "Going native" was a popular and dismissive European judgment frequently applied to those who paid attention to the local scene; for the Northwest Company it was a term of praise.

Which isn't to say that the Montreal partners, the men who returned for the winter from Grand Portage (the company inland headquarters on the west shore of Lake Superior) endured meals of crude buffalo meat and Saskatoon berries. Quite the opposite: the city's *nouveau riche* passed the long dark days over epic dinners in restaurants and taverns. They also liked masked balls and music recitals, sleigh

THE BEAVER CLUB WAS FOUNDED IN 1785 BY MONTREAL-BASED MEMBERS OF THE NORTHWEST COMPANY. IN THE EARLY YEARS, THE CLUB PROVIDED A VENUE — AND A PRETENSE — FOR SEASONED FUR TRADERS TO GATHER OVER FOOD AND GENEROUS LIBATIONS. ABOVE: A RETIREMENT PARTY AT THE BEAVER CLUB IN THE QUEEN ELIZABETH HOTEL, MONTREAL, 1960. OPPOSITE: IN SAULT STE MARIE, THE NORTH WEST COMPANY DEVELOPED A FISHERY FOR THE FUR TRADE, AND DUG A CANAL TO MOVE CANOES AND BOATS.

# Ingenuity, courage, and some luck saw them through the Rockies and the less harrowing coastal range.

## AGILE, MOBILE AND MERCANTILE

*When it first went into business in the late 1770s, the Northwest Company competed with the HBC by attacking its main weakness — immobility. The Bay conducted business out of permanent trading posts at river mouths and other key locations across the north. And because these posts were hundreds of miles apart, aboriginal customers had to travel long distances to swap their pelts for wares. What began as a convenience for the HBC was an ongoing inconvenience for its customers, and the Northwest Company exploited this opportunity by detouring past the HBC posts and delivering trade goods to natives in the interior of the country. NWC traders were the nation's first traveling salesmen.*

*The Northwest Company's business plan was highly effective but labour intensive. A stationary HBC trading post could be staffed by a handful of employees. A canoe brigade required many more hands — in 1800 the NWC had about 1,300 people on its payroll (compared to approximately 6,900 today.) The Hudson's Bay Company ran its entire North American empire with only 500 employees.*

... the value, or instrument ...

—house, (2) the ... here, the Beaver Lyes within the ...
are Disturb'd, or has a mind they ...

ALEXANDER MACKENZIE (BELOW) COMPLETED THE FIRST EAST-WEST JOURNEY ACROSS CANADA IN 1793. AT THE END OF HIS TRIP, MACKENZIE MARKED HIS ACHIEVEMENT IN REDDISH PAINT MADE OF VERMILION AND BEAR GREASE ON A ROCK (OPPOSITE). LATER, SURVEYORS PERMANENTLY INSCRIBED HIS WORDS INTO THE ROCK.

rides and card tournaments. In 1785 a group of them founded the Beaver Club, a supper/drinking club that was soon notorious for its soirees, which often ended when the last man passed out. Membership was initially limited to fur traders who had survived at least one full season running a trading post in *le pays d'en haut*. Interestingly, though Simon McTavish had traveled inland several times to inspect operations, and chaired the annual general meeting at Grand Portage, he had never wintered over. As such, the company boss couldn't fully appreciate the club's motto: "Fortitude in Distress." Eight years into the Beaver Club's existence they wisely relented, admitting McTavish to the group.

Simon McTavish was the archetypal free trader, Peter Pond the pioneering intrepid explorer. The extraordinary Alexander Mackenzie proved a unique cross of these two aspects of the company's character. Having apprenticed under Pond, Mackenzie was just 28 when, posted in Athabasca country, he too set out to seek a route to the Pacific. He had in mind elevating the Northwest Company from an assembly of regional fur traders to, in a sense, a global corporation able to expand its business to the Orient. Luckily, such boldness of vision was aligned with a voyageur's brawn. A proud, stubborn Scotsman with a domineering nature, Mackenzie had a reputation for superhuman feats of endurance. Legend has him snowshoeing hundreds of miles for a Christmas dinner and paddling a canoe for three days into frigid headwinds, without rest. He also fathered children with native women before settling down in his middle years with a much younger Scottish girl.

But before Mackenzie became a family man, he achieved what no European had managed: to cross the continent by land. (His forays preceded the better-known 1805 Lewis and Clark expedition to the Pacific by 13 years.) In early June of 1789 Mackenzie set off with a four-canoe crew to fulfill Pond's dream. In his pockets were rubles for presumed contact with Russians across the ocean. Following Peter Pond's inaccurate map, the crew ended up paddling more north than west, reaching the Beaufort Sea, and the Arctic Ocean, via the river now bearing his name. By halfway, Mackenzie knew he wasn't likely to use that Russian currency. Still, he insisted on completing the journey, under enormous hardship, only to immediately turn around and paddle back down to Fort Chipewyan. One hundred and two days and three thousand miles, for no reward.

Four years later, armed with better information from natives and the spur of a £20,000 reward by British Parliament for the discovery of the Northwest Passage, Mackenzie tried again. Leaving in May this time, his crew, featuring two aboriginal guides, traced the Peace River west to the Rockies. The awesome sight of these huge, snow-capped mountains raised the question: how to penetrate the whitewater river canyons and sheer gorges that provided the only access further west? Ingenuity, courage and some luck saw them through the Rockies and the less harrowing coastal range, until finally Alexander Mackenzie laid

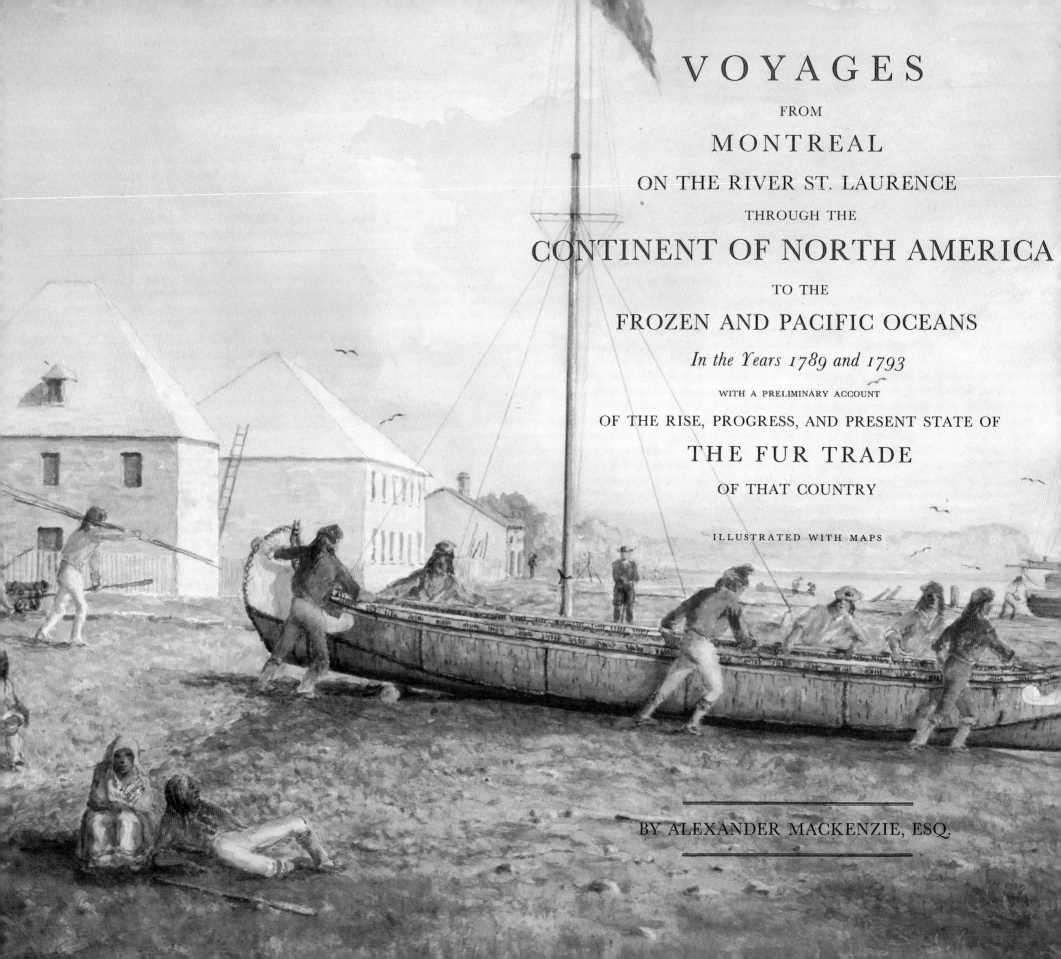

# VOYAGES

FROM

## MONTREAL

ON THE RIVER ST. LAURENCE

THROUGH THE

## CONTINENT OF NORTH AMERICA

TO THE

## FROZEN AND PACIFIC OCEANS

*In the Years 1789 and 1793*

WITH A PRELIMINARY ACCOUNT

OF THE RISE, PROGRESS, AND PRESENT STATE OF

## THE FUR TRADE

OF THAT COUNTRY

ILLUSTRATED WITH MAPS

BY ALEXANDER MACKENZIE, ESQ.

"The Company became the fledgling nation's original corporation, and the foundation for its lasting commercial establishment."

eyes upon the gigantic cedar and hemlock trees of the Pacific rain forest. Bella Coola Indians welcomed the explorers, who could now taste salt in the air. Obliged by the arrival of a less friendly rival native tribe, Mackenzie made a quick departure after hastily painting a rock in Dean Sound with a memorial to their fleeting presence.

The next morning the crew turned around and retraced their steps. Thirty-three days, 2,811 miles, back to the fort, but this time with entirely different results. "Here my voyages of discovery terminate," Mackenzie wrote in his journal. "Their toils and their dangers, their solicitudes and sufferings, have not been exaggerated in my description." For his efforts, the exhausted explorer suffered some kind of nervous breakdown.

Alexander Mackenzie would recover, and go on to publish a best-selling 550-page account of those voyages. He would also briefly part ways and even compete with the Northwest Company. His dispute would be in part over business differences with Simon McTavish regarding the economic logic of exploration — neither of Mackenzie's expeditions, financed by his trading partners, contributed a single pelt to any warehouse — and in part due to the clash of two egos. But for the moment, this fragile partnership of trading upstarts was a startling success. Within 20 years of its formation the company dominated the HBC and controlled nearly 80 percent of Canadian fur sales. A typical year brought in some hundred thousand beaver skins, and nearly that many again in muskrat, marten, mink, lynx, fox, otter, bear and buffalo. Profits were huge for the Montreal partners — unlike the HBC, neither profits, nor those earning them, left for England at the end of the season — and with their often spectacular returns they commissioned and constructed the city's first great mansions along Sherbrooke Street. The Company became the fledgling nation's original corporation, and the foundation for its lasting commercial establishment.

## TRADE WARS AND BUSINESS MERGERS

The Nor'westers almost didn't survive far into the new century. The break between McTavish and Mackenzie, initiated during the annual meeting of partners in 1799, ballooned into a civil war, with the remaining stakeholders taking sides. By 1802 the situation was dire. Despite the efforts of McTavish to revamp the surviving partnership, by expanding operations and raising its share capital as a way to reward veteran traders who would confront the upstart competition, the rival Sir Alexander Mackenzie and Co. had nearly the same working capital as the NWC. It was a nasty fight, all the more so for being between former colleagues. Sir Alex, now a celebrity on both sides of the Atlantic, even tried buying their mutual rival, the HBC, offering a staggering £103,000. At the height of the hostilities, a dispute between company men at Fort de l'Isle on the Saskatchewan River resulted in a fatal shooting. Only the sudden death of Simon McTavish in July 1804 saved the feud from possibly bringing down one, or both, firms. McTavish was fifty four.

His hand-picked successor and nephew, William McGillivray, quickly negotiated a merger. So stormy and overpowering was Mackenzie, however, that the deal was reached on condition that he play no part in the newly reunited Northwest Company. Finished as an explorer, with suddenly no mechanism to forge the global trade organization he had long promoted, Alexander Mackenzie left Canada and settled back in Scotland. His death almost 20 years later occurred, it so happened, the same year the Company merged again, this time losing its name, and then its identity, to the HBC. Might the Nor'westers have thrived longer, and even become a truly international trading giant, under Mackenzie's trail-blazing stewardship? The more practical McGillivray remained Chief Director until the merger of 1821.

Simon McTavish died without seeing New Fort, the impressive replacement for

*19*

> # "We had to pass where no human being should venture."

Grand Portage. Built on the site of an abandoned French fort at the mouth of the Kaministiquia River along the northwest shore of Lake Superior, well away from the lately redrawn US border, New Fort solved the problem of having to negotiate a shifting international boundary, and the requests from US customs for fees to paddle through their territory with goods. (A number of the company's smaller trading posts had suddenly ended up inside America.) The facility had 42 buildings within a low-walled area of 225 acres — the largest trading post in North America. Within a few years it also had a proper name: Fort William, in honour of William McGillivray. There was no escaping the reality that the deeper into the continent the Nor'westers penetrated in search of untrapped territories, the harder it was to make the return journey to Montreal in a single rowing season. Fort William made it easier to store the furs during winter and to house company men, likewise stranded in the middle of the continent, in comfort.

Among those who wintered there were David Thompson and Simon Fraser. The dream of commercial exploration, still with an eye to finding a river that could serve as a transportation route all the way to the Pacific Ocean, had not died with the withdrawal of Alexander Mackenzie. These second-generation Nor'westers kept the idea alive, with the support of senior partners, including McGillivray, who more and more feared the rise of the ever expanding United States, especially now that the team of Lewis and Clark had reached the estuary of the Columbia River. If their traditional land route was cut off by another redrawn border, the company would surely fail.

Still another McTavish relation, the dour but determined Simon Fraser was entrusted to erect a series of trading posts along the Great Divide and then follow the Columbia River to its mouth. He devoted two perilous years to discovering just how untamed, and often untamable, was that western frontier. In 1808 Fraser, having established several forts, led a crew of 18 voyageurs and two Carrier native guides down what he believed was the Columbia River, hoping to ride it to the ocean. Though the rugged landscape was lovely enough to remind him of Scotland — he dubbed the region, now northern British Columbia, New Caledonia — the river itself was a nightmare. The crew had to negotiate explosive rapids, lethal whirlpools and narrow walking ledges above sheer canyons. They also faced hostile natives who hurled boulders down at them from above. A dazed Fraser reached the Pacific, only to realize by a reading of latitudes

that he was three degrees north of the Columbia. Indeed, it was another great river, now named after the Scotsman, and certainly no highway for commerce. "We had to pass where no human being should venture ... " Fraser wrote in his journal.

If Simon Fraser's journey had any business value, it was to end forever the notion that freight canoes might penetrate the Rocky Mountains to the Pacific side. But what about going around those same mountains? In the 1790s Fraser had helped poach a talented employee away from the HBC to serve as the company's chief surveyor. The Welshman David Thompson had trained as a teenager under Samuel Hearne, the English explorer, fur trader and naturalist. Hearne's 1770s overland excursions across northern Canada to the Arctic Ocean provided the HBC with its first interior trading posts and set the benchmark for journeys of discovery. By this time Thompson was in his thirties. A gifted mapmaker and geographer with a native wife and family who accompanied him on his epic wanderings and a fluency in four aboriginal languages, he took on the task of surveying the mighty Columbia. Thompson began in spring 1811 by posting a paper at the junction of the Snake and the (properly identified) Columbia, claiming the territory for Great Britain and the Northwest Company. Then he set off to discover exactly what that claim involved.

Again, the senior partners had an urgent reason to own a passage along a river corridor to the ocean. The American mogul John Jacob Astor, owner of the Great American Fur Company and the Pacific Fur Company, was pushing for the west coast. (Of much less concern was a competitor to the north. The Russian-American Company, founded in 1799, had been granted 20-year renewable charter over trade in Russian America comprising the Aleutian Islands and Alaska, sending one-third of its profits to the Russian czar.) Thompson did reach the Pacific, on July 15, but too late: Astor had arrived at the mouth of the mighty Columbia in present day Washington State three months earlier, and built a fort there.

The Northwest Company would find no toehold on the west coast then or ever. And while the explorations of Mackenzie, Fraser and Thompson had done much to establish British territorial sovereignty in the New World, it had achieved almost nothing of commercial value for those who financed them. (The expeditions helped as well to outline the future shape of Canada.) When the United States declared war on

Great Britain the following year, the Company found itself caught in the middle, with several of its posts in the direct line of fire. With the Great Lakes especially vulnerable — an NWC ship, the *Nancy*, was sunk by the Americans — Nor'westers had no choice but to once more ask their commercial enemies to use their safer routes. Any hope of a sympathetic response from a fellow British firm in wartime was soon dashed; the HBC, seeing an opportunity to wound its rival, demanded a preposterous £10,000 annual fee. The Northwest Company reluctantly stuck with their usual waterways, absorbing the risk of encountering a cannonball.

More than ever, conflicts abounded in the fur trade, many of them linked to the whim of international politics. One flashpoint was at Fort Gibraltar, the Northwest trading post built in 1809 along the bank of the Red River, near the junction of the Assiniboine, in present day Winnipeg. Just two years after the fort opened, the HBC granted the Scottish peer and philanthropist Lord Selkirk a staggering 27,454,000 hectares on which to establish a colony for Scottish and Irish immigrants seeking a better life. Selkirk, who was a major shareholder with strong family ties to the HBC, wanted in particular to address the deep poverty in the Scottish Highlands, and to make use of the vast empty spaces in the Canadian west that he had first read about in, ironically enough, the memoirs of Alexander Mackenzie. The settlement encompassed an area nearly three times the size of Scotland, including land directly across the river from Fort Gibraltar. Suspicious Nor'westers, noting how many herds of buffalo wandered those vast empty spaces, saw in the settlement a potential threat to their vital supply of pemmican. As with the loss of a waterway route, without pemmican to fuel the workhorse *voyageurs,* their business model would collapse.

They were right to be suspicious. Settlers, having traveled a full year to reach the settlement, arrived with nothing to find that no advance preparations had been made by Selkirk. Deprivation, starvation and even death by exposure — in particular for those who had the misfortune of reaching the Red River at the outset of winter — plagued the venture. Northwest Company men, often themselves Scottish, extended a hand to those poor folk, while gathering evidence that the HBC was using the Red River Settlement to cripple their enterprise. Tensions escalated when an aggressive "governor" ordered that no traders be permitted to "take out any provisions — meat, grain or vegetables

— from the Selkirk territory." This effectively banned the Metis, who earned their living manufacturing pemmican, from hunting buffalo or selling the foodstuff to the Northwest Company. When that same official, having confiscated shipments of pemmican, gave the occupants of Fort Gibraltar six months to vacate the premises — the land, he claimed, now belonged to Lord Selkirk — hostilities were inevitable.

First, inflamed Nor'westers arrested the governor. Then, having offered transport to any of Selkirk's dissatisfied settlers who wished to farm elsewhere in Manitoba, they burnt the local HBC post, Fort Douglas, to the ground. Much of 1816 was given over to skirmishes; an HBC employee sent to restore order was killed and in retaliation the HBC destroyed Fort Gibraltar. Then Metis forces, now openly aligned with the Northwest Company, confronted those who had destroyed Gibraltar, triggering a deadly gun battle. The Battle of Seven Oaks left nineteen settlers, and one Metis, dead. It also suggested that the use of force to resolve business disputes had become a viable option.

Competition between the HBC and the Northwest Company reached its climax at Fort William. On August 12, 1816, Lord Selkirk positioned a small army across the river

SAMUEL HEARNE, ENGLISH EXPLORER, FUR TRADER AND NATURALIST. HEARNE JOINED THE HUDSON'S BAY COMPANY AS A MATE ON THE SLOOP *CHURCHILL* IN FEBRUARY 1766. HE OPENED CUMBERLAND HOUSE, THE HBC'S FIRST INLAND TRADING POST, IN 1774.

from the company's frontier headquarters. A warrant for treason, conspiracy and accessory to murder was issued to none other than the fort's namesake, William McGillivray. When McGillivray and three other partners paddled to Selkirk's camp to negotiate, they were summarily arrested. That night, partners inside the fort, fearing their senior management would be put on trial for what had happened in Manitoba, began burning company records. Selkirk raided Fort William, arrested more employees and seized documents, and then bundled them all into overloaded canoes for transport to Montreal. To make matters worse, one of the canoes was swamped in a storm, killing nine Nor'westers, including a partner. Selkirk was undaunted: in a note to the governor general of Upper Canada, he assured him that he was sending "... a Cargo of Criminals ... to be tried in court." All charges were dropped, it turned out, when that cargo of criminals reached Montreal.

No question now: the fur trade in British North America was in disarray, with no one's behavior especially flattering. Forty years of entrepreneurship and risk-taking, of bold business decisions and fabulous returns, along with the history-changing, nation-building voyages of continental discovery could not assure the Northwest Company a viable future. For all the financial might of its senior partners, in the larger context of imperial power the enterprise was simply too small and vulnerable to easily survive. But for those impressive decades the company had thrived as a singular commercial force in early Canada. It had also been a progressive model, often born of necessity, for how to conduct business in a manner that engaged, not repelled, the surrounding indigenous communities, and was integrated with the landscape, rather than simply viewing it as a resource to be used until used up.

## AN ERA ENDED

William McGillivray had hoped for a full amalgamation with the HBC. But by 1821, deteriorating business conditions and in-fighting among his partners made his efforts to have the Northwest Company treated as an equal in any coalition nearly impossible. Regardless, on March 26 he signed an agreement uniting the two fur trading giants under the name the Hudson's Bay Company. (To keep the Royal Charter, they had to keep the name.) Officially, a joint board comprising equal members of both sides would oversee the sharing of capital costs and profits. The deal was sealed by summer, and Nor'westers gathering for their final general meeting at Fort William had cause for optimism. But within three years McGillivray was dead and the profit-sharing agreement had dissolved. Surviving partners lost their board votes, and soon had no say in how the HBC was run. Fort William, too, was reduced in standing to simply another HBC outpost, until it finally closed in 1883. Dozens of other posts were shut down immediately.

George Simpson, the "acting overseas governor" of the HBC, ordered the shuttering of those duplicate operations. The 33-year-old Scottish Simpson, who visited Canada for the first time on accepting the position, displayed some of the disposition of a Nor'wester, most notably in his capacity for hard work and his willingness to put aside the comforts of Montreal for the vast field of operations, where his surprise visits to Company posts became legendary. But Simpson ran the overseas operation of a British corporation that remained based in London, not only for the duration of his distinguished career, but for a full seven decades into the 20th century. Neither he, nor his successors, could ever be quite so firmly on the Canadian ground, either as businessmen or simply as citizens.

To the casual observer the Northwest Company vanished in 1821. But for 166 years a remnant of the great enterprise thrived in the gargantuan HBC. If any dimension of the Hudson's Bay Company's North American operations kept the spirit of the Nor'westers alive, and indeed the link to the founding enterprising character of the Canadian north west, it was the northern stores, a network of more than two hundred small shops serving remote, still barely accessible communities across the same northern regions explored and mapped by Samuel Hearne and Alexander Mackenzie. In these often modest stores and harsh circumstances — an afterthought in the HBC business plan, despite being highly profitable — people gathered, as they had done at those vanished trading posts, to exchange goods, news and gossip, as well as to pick up necessities. Often the outlets retained the name of a post, harkening back to their uses during the glorious, outsized fur trade era and in recognition of an active and substantial fur trading business, right into the 1950s.

The HBC's northern stores kept the legend and lore of the Northwest Company alive until a small group of savvy entrepreneurs would come forward with the proposition that the bold vision of the original company, embodied in spirit by these enduring throwbacks to an earlier age, was a remarkable fit with the rapidly changing commercial landscape of late-20th-century Canada.

### CHAPTER ONE

# REBIRTH OF A COMPANY

# WE LIKED IT BECAUSE IT WAS SUCH A GRAND CANADIAN INSTITUTION, AND IT WAS PARTICULARLY ATTRACTIVE BECAUSE IT HAD BEEN FINANCIALLY VIABLE FOR SO MANY YEARS AND WAS A DISCREET ENTITY WITHIN THE BAY EMPIRE.

OPPOSITE: Hudson's Bay Company store in Prince Rupert, B.C., officially opened August 14, 1975, and was typical of HBC's expansion into rural centres during the 1970s. The store occupies 48,000 square feet and cost approximately $5 million to build. FAR RIGHT: Earl Boon. PREVIOUS PAGE: A rural Hudson's Bay Company store in 1953.

Long before the arrival of the Royal Canadian Mounted Police, before the influx of nursing stations and schoolteachers and snowmobiles, the sole foothold of European civilization in the Canadian north was the Hudson's Bay Company trading post. For almost the entire first 300 years, the HBC network of northern stores served as a sort of de facto national government. Consider that the country's first currency was the finished beaver pelt, (the "Made Beaver" or "MB") and that the symbols of the northern store network — the Point blanket, the checkered wool jacket, the snowshoe, the cedar canoe — have grown into symbols of Canada itself.

On the surface it was a business. The northern stores provided food staples and hardware to aboriginal trappers in return for high-quality furs. But it wasn't just a business for the individuals involved in the day-to-day functioning of the store. It was an enterprise fueled by desire. It wasn't money that prompted young men from Glasgow and Montreal and Winnipeg and Newfoundland to spend their lives in the north. It was love — for the stunning landscape, for the people, for the adventure of daily life. And anyone who has tried to boil water by immersing red-hot stones in a birchbark bucket will understand a trapper's desire for a new tin kettle. The northern store network functioned so well for centuries because both parties — customer and merchant — were avid participants in the partnership.

It took a certain sort of individual to run a northern trading post. It required devotion, honour, ingenuity and hard work. Those values might sound quaint in the classrooms of today's business schools, but loyalty and personal integrity were considered mandatory personality traits of a 20th-century HBC northern store manager.

Earl Boon grew up in Montreal and joined the Hudson's Bay Company as a young man. In 1954 he took a clerking job on the company supply ship *Rupertsland*, delivering freight to northern stores in Labrador. "I just loved it," he says. "The country was spectacular, and the people were really special. The HBC people were war veterans, for the most part, and had come home with a deep understanding of what they had been fighting for. There were no contracts or legal documents required. Agreements were confirmed with a handshake. A man's word was all you needed."

Boon quickly fell into what he calls the "brotherhood" of the

| 1986 | JANUARY 1987 | JANUARY 1987 |
|---|---|---|
| Initial meeting with Iain Ronald puts $180-million offer on table. | Jim Oborne brought in. | Derek Riley named Chairman of the Board of Directors. |

northern trading post network and began working his way up. (He eventually became vice president of merchandising.) He says the old handshake ethics of the northern store network began fading in the 1970s, challenged and replaced by the harder-nosed values of the modern era.

The economy was expanding, and resource towns such as Labrador City, Prince Rupert, Thompson and Yellowknife were growing like hungry teenagers. The Hudson's Bay Company chased these new markets by building midsize department stores in larger rural centres. In the early 1980s, when a serious recession hit the North American economy, the company realized it had grown too quickly. "The Bay lost $22 million in 1981," says Boon. We had taken on too much. Interest rates were high, sales were down, and we were in big trouble."

Like many observers, Boon believed that the company had to reassess its strategy and in his words, "take a knife and cut out what was wrong." He says that in its eagerness to grow with

Canada's population, The Bay invested millions into its more southern department stores, largely ignoring the northern division. Buildings up north were deteriorating, and there had been half-hearted attempts to integrate purchasing and supply systems with the Zellers department store chain, which The Bay had acquired as part of its rapid expansion at that time. Boon and many others recommended keeping the northern store network as a stand-alone entity, and The Bay's senior executives agreed. "This was a very important moment in the history of the northern stores," he says. "Because of that decision, we became our own master. We became, for all purposes, a separate company within the larger corporation of The Bay. If that hadn't happened, I don't think we could ever have broken away and risen on our own two feet."

A Toronto businessman named Ian Sutherland was observing these rather serious goings-on at The Bay with more than idle interest. "I had always followed the northern stores," he says. "Not just as an investor, but because I had a personal interest in the stores."

**JANUARY 28, 1987**
Deal to buy the Hudson's Bay
(HBC) Northern Stores division
is closed.

**JANUARY 28, 1987**
Northern Stores
name registered.

**MAY 2, 1987**
Nonsuch party held, including transfer
ceremony of the Hudson's Bay Northern
Stores to NWC.

BECAUSE OF MY DAD'S LONG HISTORY WITH THE BAY, THERE WAS SOMETHING OF A BOND OF TRUST BETWEEN IAIN RONALD AND ME. I FOUND HIM TO BE A VERY DECENT INDIVIDUAL — FAIR, BALANCED AND DOWN-TO-EARTH.

## BUILDING A DEAL

His father, Hugh Sutherland, had once managed the northern store network, and company magazines *The Beaver* and *The Moccasin Telegraph* were always lying around the Sutherland home. "The fur trading posts were part of our family history, and I would recognize many of the people in the photographs when I read the magazines," he says. When Sutherland was 15, his dad got him a job at the Hudson's Bay store in Minaki, a village in northwestern Ontario, and that summer experience set the hook. "I loved that job," he says. "It was my first time out of the house, on my own. At noon, I would swim across the bay to have lunch at a fishing lodge, then I would swim back to work in the store for the rest of the afternoon."

He got a commerce degree from the University of Manitoba and worked in banking in Toronto for a number of years. By 1986, he had helped foster the growth of a small company into a multi-million-dollar firm called Mutual Trust, and was keeping an eye out, as always, for investment opportunities. His brother-in-law, Jeff Gidney, was a full-time graduate of the northern stores' management program and had moved on to become a successful Canadian Tire dealer. Together, they began to imagine the possibility of buying The Bay's northern division. "We liked it because it was such a grand Canadian institution, and it was particularly attractive because it had been financially sound for so many years and was run as a discrete entity within the HBC empire."

Sutherland finally "got up the courage" to phone Iain Ronald, the senior vice president responsible for The Bay's NSD Investment, as the Northern Stores Division was known, and make the pitch. After mulling it over with his colleagues, Ronald called back and said he was interested in the concept. "Four of us went in to see him," says Sutherland. "It was David Broadhurst, my partner Ray Dore, Jeff Gidney and me. Because of my dad's long history with The Bay, there was something of a bond of trust between Iain Ronald and me. I found him to be a very decent individual — fair, balanced and down-to-earth. At the same time, there was no mistaking that he was a man accustomed to calling the shots. When he named his price — $180 million — it was quite clear he was not open to haggling or bargaining."

Sutherland says the price was "a little higher" than they expected, but he left the meeting with a feeling of excitement. "I know how to raise money, and I immediately began contacting potential investors."

Unfortunately for Sutherland, a business reporter heard about the meeting and assumed that Sutherland was representing Mutual Trust in the negotiation. A headline in the *Globe and Mail* immediately announced Mutual Life acquires HBC's Northern Stores. In Sutherland's words "that's when all hell broke loose."

He and Ray Dore had not advised their parent company what they were doing, and over that weekend, some of the company's outside directors called the CEO of Mutual Life at his home, asking for details. Despite this awkward development, Sutherland's

I HAD REDUCED MY INTEREST IN MUTUAL TRUST IN 1985 AND WAS ABLE TO SELL OTHER INVESTMENTS AND BORROW ENOUGH TO INVEST OVER $1 MILLION BY REMORTGAGING OUR HOME. MY WIFE, JUDY, WENT ALONG WITH IT, AS USUAL. WE WERE RISKING ALL WE OWNED BUT MY WIFE AGREED IT LOOKED LIKE A SOUND INVESTMENT.

proposal still looked viable because Mutual Life's investment department actually liked the concept. "They chose to be our lead institutional investor at $2.5 million," says Sutherland, "which gave them a 7 percent position. Mutual Trust then committed $3 million (600,000 shares) on its own account and $1.275 million from its RSP accounts, company officers and family members."

Sutherland says he and his brother-in-law Jeff Gidney then pooled their resources and invested $3.8 million (10.9 percent) in a holding company called Paint Lake Investments. "Since he was a successful Canadian Tire dealer Jeff was able to raise his share from his bank," recalls Sutherland. "I had reduced my interest in Mutual Trust in 1985 and was able to sell other investments and borrow enough to invest over $1 million by remortgaging our home. My wife, Judy, went along with it, as usual. We were risking all we owned, but she agreed that it looked like a sound investment."

Sutherland then enlisted the support of Peter Churchill-Smith, a vice president at Mutual Trust, and they approached "many potential investors," including pension funds, life insurance companies and Mutual Trust's clients. The response from some was encouraging. "We approached TD Bank and asked for an operating loan of $85 million," says Sutherland. "Within two weeks, they not only approved the operating loan, they approved a term loan of $40 million and subscribed for 400,000 shares ($2 million) of the equity."

Just prior to closing, Sutherland says they were still short. "Mutual Trust was the investment banker for the deal, and we — Mutual that is — still needed a little over $1 million. Central Capital was close to approving the investment but didn't want to release the money until after the closing. So we needed a bridge loan, which Jeff agreed to guarantee, and once again, I had to tell Judy that we might have to move our three boys into a rental townhouse and sell our home if we couldn't repay the bridge loan. Fortunately, Peter Cole at Central Capital approved the $2 million investment. Our bridge loan was repaid and we didn't lose our house."

Some of the private and institutional investors Sutherland approached have their own interesting perspective on the high-

**DECEMBER 1989**
Edward Kennedy hired as Director
of Corporate Development and
Legal Counsel.

**1990**
Northern Stores retail
banner rolled out.

stakes, enterprising bravado required in putting the acquisition deal together. One of those private investors was Derek Riley. Today, Riley is a tall, handsome individual with a full head of silver hair who, at the age of 90, still jogs regularly and could no doubt work as a model for one of those *New Yorker* ads promoting the rewards of a well-planned retirement portfolio. A former Olympian who competed in the two-man rowing trials in Helsinki ("We didn't do all that well in the competition because the hull of our boat was wrecked on the way overseas"), he came out of the Royal Canadian Navy in 1945 with what he describes as "no business skills whatsoever."

Riley started his career at Peat Marwick as an accountant and worked on the ongoing audit of the Hudson's Bay Company's northern stores, which then operated under the name of the Fur Trade Department. It was the 1950s, but in the far north it might just as well have been the 1850s. Many aboriginal people still lived off the land, in hand-hewn log cabins during the winter and "under canvas" in the summer, and fur trapping was an important part of their lifestyle. Across the north, Hudson's Bay trading post employees still traded food staples, clothing and hardware for high-quality winter pelts.

Along with the qualities of loyalty and honesty, HBC traders had to cultivate a keen eye for the subtle qualities of a beaver, mink or fox pelt. If an HBC trader paid too much for a load of furs, their notoriously tight-fisted supervisors wouldn't be pleased. If they paid too little, their aboriginal customers might take their business elsewhere. (Despite the common — and condescending — stereotype of the innocent native being exploited by traders offering coloured beads and trinkets, native trappers were quite capable of taking care of themselves. At one northern store, a trader bought a load of arctic fox pelts and sent them out on the next ship. The ship ran aground and the cargo became salvage, so the trappers rescued their pelts and sold them to the HBC manager all over again.) The chief financial officer for the Fur Trade Department was then Ian Sutherland's father, Hugh. The senior Sutherland liked Riley's firm

The *Winnipeg Free Press* ran the headline "Northern Fortunes Shine" with a 1989 article about the flourishing NWC chain. Derek Riley (left) was the chairman and the interim CEO at the time. PREVIOUS SPREAD: Ian Sutherland, who would transform the Bay's Northern Stores division, was born for the job. His father, Hugh Sutherland (pictured at right), was once the CFO for the Fur Trade Department, and ran the company magazines, including the *Moccasin Telegraph*.

31

>>

**1990**
Enterprise 95 is created as a five-year roadmap to steer NWC's business northward and towards becoming the leader in serving remote communities.

**1990**
NWC installs point-of-sale store technology to better capture sales data and improve merchandise productivity.

character and his zesty energy and decided to lure him away from Peat Marwick. "How would you like to come and work for us in the Hudson's Bay Fur Trade Department?"

"I asked him the first question on any young husband's mind," says Riley. "How much will you pay me? He offered me exactly twice what I was being paid at Peat Marwick, so that's how I became a Bay man."

Riley recalls that "Hugh Sutherland transferred to Montreal, and R.H. 'Bob' Cheshire became my general manager. Mr. Cheshire was quite a strict and formal individual who never called me anything but 'Riley,' and I in turn never called him anything but 'Mr. Cheshire.' If you came up with a suggestion for improving things they'd say 'well, put it down on paper.' You'd write it all out, make it interesting,

and then it'd get into somebody's inbox and that'd be the last you heard of it. No response whatsoever. I found that pretty frustrating. So I quit, and bought my own little company — a glorified blacksmith shop — and built it up and sold it and made some good money out of it. Then I became a director of a number of companies and became pretty well-connected with the Winnipeg business community. The years went by and it was in the late 1980s when something happened that brought me full circle back to the HBC northern store business."

Riley says that Ian Sutherland came to see him on the advice of his father. "Ian was looking for someone who knew the HBC's northern fur business, because he and his brother-in-law Jeff Gidney had cooked up this plan to buy the northern stores from

**1990**
Planning begins for a new distribution centre to serve NWC Canada stores with cutting-edge technology and processes.

**JANUARY 1990**
Northern Stores Inc. changes its name to The North West Company Inc. (NWC) and formally repatriates one of Canada's greatest business legacies.

THE ECONOMY WAS AILING AND THE BAY WAS HAVING SO MANY GODDAMN PROBLEMS WITH THEIR BIG STORES THAT THE POSTS WERE BEING NEGLECTED. IN PARTICULAR THEY HADN'T DONE ANYTHING TO UPGRADE THEIR POINT-OF-SALE EQUIPMENT, WHERE YOU CAN REALLY CONTROL INVENTORY, USING COMPUTERS AND SO FORTH.

The Bay. I listened to Ian's pitch and thought it was an intriguing idea. The economy was ailing and The Bay was having so many goddamn problems with their big stores that the posts were being neglected. In particular they hadn't done anything to upgrade their point-of-sale equipment, where you can really control inventory, using computers and so forth. Ian Sutherland told me that he had gone to see Iain Ronald and had offered to buy the northern stores. Sutherland had acquired loans from several large institutions and The Bay had agreed to carry some of the mortgage, but they still needed to raise $35 million in equity, of which they had managed to assemble $22 million. So they were short about $13 million. I told him I liked the deal, and I would go out and find $10 million for him.

"I'd rather not mention his name," continues the ever gentlemanly Riley, "but I contacted this fellow who was the CEO of a large local investment firm." The executive (let's call him The CEO) listened to Riley's pitch and agreed to throw in $5 million. Then Riley called an acquaintance at United Canadian Shares, who on the strength of the CEO's participation agreed to put in another $5 million. "I put in some of my own money and that got us close enough to a done deal," Riley says. "We threw a party at the Manitoba Museum aboard the HMS *Nonsuch*, the old replica wooden ship that goes back to the founding of the Hudson's Bay Company. Everyone was clapping and it was a great historic event. Then we had a couple of meetings that were a bit contentious, having to do with local control of the company and a few other touchy issues. But everyone was quite excited and things were progressing nicely. Then, right after one of these meetings, I was walking down Broadway Avenue with this distinguished executive and he said, 'I'm out.' I was flabbergasted, of course, and asked him why."

"I don't like the management."

"Oh please, this is a wonderful franchise," responded Riley. "If the management is not good, we can always replace it."

The CEO refused to budge. Furthermore, he called Bob Jones, the chairman of United Canadian Shares, and convinced him that he shouldn't get involved either. "So I went from champ to chump in a very short time," says Riley. "We were suddenly short 10 million bucks. And it was potentially very embarrassing because we had made this big announcement, named these fellows as directors, and so on. Fortunately, Jim Oborne got involved. At that point it was Oborne who really made it work."

OPPOSITE: On the brink of a deal to buy The Bay's Northern Stores, Ian Sutherland, Jeff Gidney and Derek Riley (far right) threw a party aboard a replica of the HMS *Nonsuch* at the Manitoba Museum, May 1987. FAR LEFT: President and CEO of the Northern Stores Marvin E. Tiller presents a beaver pelt to HBC Govenor Donald S. McGiverin on behalf of the Northern Stores at "The End of an Era" dinner party. The party, given by HBC to say thank you to the Northern Stores Division for 317 years of service, was held on April 15, 1987, at the Manitoba Club.

33

MARCH 1990
NWC acquires *Aivik*, a 470,000-cubic-foot, ice-class container vessel and the first ship of its type in the Arctic.

1991
NWC introduces branded quick-service food in select stores.

1991
NWC launches Healthy Living and Stay in School programs in northern communities.

>>

## SCENES FROM THE OLD NORTH

*In The North West Company archives there are dozens of binders brimming with photographs and handwritten notes, identifying places and people in the old network of Hudson's Bay Northern Stores that served communities strung across more than half of Canada. Many HBC posts are represented in this collection, with some small, cracked and faded images dating as far back as the 1920s and 1930s. It's a rich narrative, evoking an era, a place and a culture that is rapidly changing as the North modernizes. These few images selected from the binders are a small taste of a life and time nearly gone, when Canada's North was like another country.*

The Hudson's Bay Northern Stores provided food staples and hardware to small communities in stunning locales. LEFT TO RIGHT: A post manager's house near the Georges River, Ungava District, Quebec; a northern BC store, 1951; Fort Ross, Somerset Island, 1946; Western Post Division, Goldfields, 1951; Fort Selkirk, YT, store; closing a post, 1955.

IT WASN'T MONEY THAT PROMPTED YOUNG MEN, AND LATER ON YOUNG WOMEN, TO COME NORTH. IT WAS LOVE FOR THE STUNNING LANDSCAPE, THE WONDERFUL PEOPLE AND THE SHEER ADVENTURE THAT EACH DAY MIGHT BRING.

THE NORTHERN STORES HAD BEEN IN BUSINESS FOR SOME 300 YEARS. IT EVEN HAS STAND-ALONE MANAGEMENT. HOW MANY OPPORTUNITIES DO YOU GET TO INVEST IN SOMETHING LIKE THAT?

## CROSSING THE FINISH LINE

Jim Oborne was born in Calgary (or as he puts it, "I met my mother there"), grew up in Toronto and attended an exclusive private school in southern Ontario. He studied at McGill in Montreal, where he assumed he would end up practicing law. "I never thought I'd wind up in the investment business," he says. "I regarded it as far too boring. Then I got a summer job in Montreal working for my dad's competitor. Their bond messenger had just been run over by a car, so I got his job. Nobody would have insured me if they'd known how Montreal cab drivers saw pedestrians running across the street as sporting targets. Anyway, I got into the research department halfway through the summer and loved it. I knew exactly what I wanted to do, and after graduation and a two-year training program I ended up with a career in the investment business."

Despite his father's advice to stay in so-called "Central Canada" young Oborne then moved to Winnipeg, where he came to enjoy working alongside "the decent people who worked for the city's large financial institutions." He also enjoyed the province's permanent sunshine, excellent golf courses, abundant lakes and forests, and world-famous waterfowl hunting. ("There is no place in North America with better duck hunting.") In Winnipeg, he built a good reputation as an investment dealer and branch manager, and by 1987 was also handling about $400 million for the Manitoba Teachers Pension Fund (what he refers to as his night job).

That's when he heard about the Northern Stores deal. "Ian Sutherland actually talked to my secretary treasurer first, who then brought the deal to me. I was interested in diversifying our pension fund with some venture capital projects, and this seemed like an excellent opportunity. I mean, the northern stores had been in business for some 300 years. It even had stand-alone management. How many opportunities do you get to invest in something like that?"

Oborne was an amateur historian, and thought of the Northern Stores as nothing less than the old Northwest Company, operating like a sleeper network within the massive organization of The Bay. "If you know your history, the Northwest Company has always been a discrete entity, even though their northern stores merged with the Hudson's Bay Company in 1821. Those northern stores still enjoyed a formidable market advantage, in that there were so many barriers

38

1991
NWC begins to sell or close 26 junior department stores that do not fit the company's focus on remote markets.

1992
*Tomorrow Store* concept launched: 42 Northern Stores are built or remodeled over the next five years at the cost of $50 million.

to new competitors. To duplicate all those little community stores at a massive investment price — why would anybody ever want to do it?"

The fact that Derek Riley supported the deal meant a lot to Oborne. "I didn't know Derek very well, except by reputation, but he was known to be an excellent businessman and a solid guy. Lots of presence, Olympic rower and all that. So I called him up and said, 'Are you putting your own money in?' He said, 'Yes, every cent I've got.' So I said, 'That's good enough for me. I'll put in $5 million.'"

Oborne then called a good friend who was managing the government pension plans of Saskatchewan, and his friend indicated he would be in for $6 million. "Then everybody chipped in a little more, including my father, brother and some friends of mine, and Sutherland in Winnipeg and Montreal and Toronto, and we had a deal."

Oborne says he and other stakeholders insisted that the chairman of the board be Derek Riley. "That was both a character and a capability thing. We all wanted to keep our Toronto and Montreal investors in line, and to do that we needed strong influence by Winnipeg and Saskatchewan investors, and of course Derek would guarantee that."

Other parties piled into the deal and helped make it work. Ian Sutherland says the TD Bank deserves a lot of credit. "We approached several banks but we were overwhelmed by TD, represented by David Scoon, who put together an all-encompassing deal in a few weeks. We later found out that Peter Purdue, a VP of credit, and Dick Thomson, the Bank's CEO, (both former Winnipeggers) knew and respected HBC and Northern Stores, and helped with the credit approval. It was a pleasant surprise for all of us that Northern Stores was portrayed as a 'featured corporate relationship' in TD's next annual report."

Not all the players were large companies and financial institutions. One of the U.K.-based directors of the Hudson's Bay Company was thrilled by the news that the northern store network was going out on its own. Sir Martin Jacombe was chair of a large U.K. investment bank, Barclay's Zoet Velde. As Sutherland recalls, "Sir Martin came to see Ray Dore and me in Toronto. He told us of his attachment and respect for the northern stores management and business, and said he wanted to remain connected with the company. Then he pulled out his cheque book and wrote out a cheque for $150,000 on the spot."

And finally, in a vote of confidence just as significant as the millions of dollars thrown in by large investors, 415 employees borrowed or used their savings to become shareholders in their new employer. It was hoped that the employees might contribute $3 million, but their eventual contribution totaled $6 million. These everyday managers and employees knew the northern stores best, and Sutherland, Riley, Oborne and the other founders were encouraged by this show of support.

On June 19, 1987, the deal closed. The Bay got its $180 million, some of it in the form of a promissory note, convertible into shares of the new entity. And the northern stores sprang to life as an independent company, albeit one that had already been conducting its affairs under various flags since 1668.

As Ian Sutherland put it, "Hudson's Bay Northern Stores was a substantial enterprise, with sales exceeding $360,000,000. But this was also an important deal in historic terms. Northern Stores Division was going back to its roots. The Hudson's Bay Company's ownership was in some ways only a legal nicety. The essence of the Northern Store's history resided in its employees, with its posts and stores, and its long-standing relationship with the people of the north."

The author Peter C. Newman once called The Hudson's Bay Company "the oldest continuous commercial enterprise still in existence." Ian Sutherland put it this way: "When our deal concluded, Hudson's Bay still retained its venerable charter, but Northern Stores Inc. retained its unique history and the future of the north."

Jim Oborne sporting "typical director wear" for board meetings in Alaska, September 1998. In 1987, Oborne convinced friends and family to support Ian Sutherland and Derek Riley's bid to buy the northern store network from the Bay. His confidence in Riley made the deal happen.

**1992**
Alaska Commercial Company (ACC) and Frontier Expediters are purchased.

**1993**
In-store training and development program launched.

**1993**
First Tomorrow Stores open in Nelson House and Easterville, Manitoba.

>>

CHAPTER TWO

# THE FIRST YEARS

AS A BRAND NEW COMPANY THAT COULD TRACE ITS
ROOTS BACK 300 YEARS, IT NEEDED TO DEFINE A NEW PATH
FOR ITSELF WITHOUT LOSING TRACK OF THE CORE VALUES
THAT HAD MADE IT SUCCESSFUL FOR SO MANY YEARS.

At the early board meetings of what was now called Northern Stores Inc., there was much debate about fundamental questions of strategy and management. As a brand new company with such a rich heritage there was a unique need to define a path without losing track of the core values that had made it successful for so many years.

One of The Bay's stipulations was that the new owners would retain the management team that ran the store network. This was of course a loyal gesture by Bay executive Iain Ronald — who made it clear that he would walk away from the deal if the interests of the employees weren't protected — but it was perhaps inevitable that the new owners would want changes to the team to go with a new name and new direction.

Marv Tiller had run Northern Stores for The Bay and stayed on through the transition period with the new owners. He was a great promoter of the company and what it had stood for. But as a new vision began to take hold, the need for a personnel change at the top became apparent.

Jim Oborne says they first looked for someone internally who could take over as CEO. "We had some very good guys, no question, but in the board's view, we needed somebody fresh. The

fur business was long gone; we were going to have to develop general merchandising and food marketing strategies for the decade ahead, as many of our markets were being affected by new competition of one form or another. People were ordering goods by phone or mail and bypassing their local merchant. Roads were getting built, and as soon as there was a new road in place our customers were off and running. So, we went through a long search and ended up interviewing a guy by the name of Ralph Trott."

## A NEW KID IN TOWN

Ralph Trott grew up in a family of 13 kids, and says they were poor enough that "eating every day was our first priority. I remember a time when we only had nine chicken drumsticks for 10 kids, and we had to figure out which of us couldn't have one. I was about 10 years old, and I remember telling my dad that one day I would make enough money that every person in my family would get their own drumstick."

As a self-described "hippie teenager," Trott hitchhiked across Canada and the United States and worked at odd jobs. He then tried university but it didn't work out. "Besides my poor family

1993
Ralph Trott resigns as
President and CEO.

1993
Ian Sutherland appointed
President and CEO.

1993
NWC receives Retail Council of
Canada award for Innovative Retailer
of the Year.

background, I felt inadequate because of my lack of education. But I joined Canadian Tire when I was 24 and that's when I realized I was good at something. I was in the purchasing and marketing area and I accelerated up through the ranks fairly quickly because I liked assembling teams that ran hard and weren't afraid of new things. By the late 1980s I was the vice president of the automotive division in Toronto — their largest purchasing and marketing division."

Jeff Gidney, a founding investor of the Northern Stores deal, was also a Canadian Tire dealer and passed Trott's name to the recruitment team. "I met with Derek Riley and the other members of the selection committee in Toronto," Trott says. "I was 39 at the time, full of brash energy and new ideas, and they were looking for that kind of person to fire up the business. My impression was that they had taken on a very antiquated company that really needed revitalizing."

OPPOSITE: Marv Tiller, 1979. THIS PAGE: Ralph Trott meets the staff at The North West Company Office with Earl Boon, 1989. PREVIOUS: Trott and Derek Riley speed towards a new era of success.

**1993**
*Quickstop* convenience outlets launched: KFC in Nelson House, Manitoba, and Pizza Hut Express in Cross Lake, Manitoba.

**JANUARY 1993**
*Selections* catalogues, in Greenlandic and Danish, are launched in Greenland. Twenty thousand catalogues distributed.

>>

# LIFE UP NORTH

*Don Coles grew up in Newfoundland and, after graduating from high school, realized that there wasn't much chance that his father could afford to send him to university in St. John's. So he applied for work as a trainee in the Hudson's Bay Company northern store network. "They sent me to Kuujjuaq, in arctic Quebec," he says. "I was supposed to work there for three years with no vacations or other breaks."*

*After a year and a half "learning the ropes" in Kuujjuaq, Coles was transferred to Salluit on the northern tip of Quebec. There wasn't much point in pining for his family and friends because there was nothing he could do about it. "There were no telephones, no scheduled airlines and no services whatsoever. Salluit was a very, very isolated community and it served as the mother home of three other stores. This was in the era before money had reached the north, so these stores were strictly trading posts, where merchandise was traded for fur and other goods. Most of the Inuit lived outside the community, in hunting camps up and down the coast. So I would often travel 180 miles down the coast to Kangirsuk. I'd go with an Inuit guide and we'd travel by dog team during the winter months and by boat in the summer."*

*His travels to the remote camps and villages would take him out on the land for extended periods of time. "The longest trip was 25 days and the shortest was about nine. We'd make camp in late afternoon and build an igloo. It was a lot colder in those days than it is today. It would get down to 40 or 50 below — that's Fahrenheit, of course — so we would be kind of happy to get into that igloo at night."*

*They used a kerosene-powered Primus stove to cook and to stay warm. "It was a one-burner and once you got it going you could strip down to a T-shirt within a couple of hours. After we ate we would let the fire go out and get into a really heavy sleep, and it was fine."*

*They carried walrus meat to feed the dogs and encountered quite a few polar bears. "Matter of fact, my Inuit guide shot a couple when I was traveling with him. We didn't worry about bears at night because the dogs would raise a fuss if they came anywhere near the camp. The danger of bears didn't really enter your mind because you got used to it. It was just a way of life."*

*Coles met a young woman in Salluit. "She was a schoolteacher from Alberta and she made my life a lot easier because she would bake us a bunch of donuts and beans to take on these trips. It was all frozen, of course, but at least my guide and I ate a lot better. After my three years were up, we went south on a six-month vacation and got married. Then I went on to Inukjuak, as store manager. That was a big step up. We spent five years in Inukjuak and then I was transferred to Montreal for a position as department manager in the distribution centre. It was quite a promotion. But we found that we missed the north too much; we missed the people, and our wonderful friends. So after six months I requested to go back as store manager. We went to Pangnirtung, where we spent the next 15 years."*

*Coles says people still lived on the land at the time and alcohol hadn't yet arrived. Pangnirtung, where he also served as Justice of the Peace and coroner, had very few social problems. "I think I dealt with one summary conviction in all the time I served as J.P."*

*In the latter part of Coles' career, he moved to Winnipeg and Edmonton where he became the company's vice president of distribution and transportation. He also helped persuade the company to buy its own shipping vessels. "We're still major shareholders in four ships," he says. "And they've worked out very well for us. I was very pleased when The North West Company bought Northern Stores from The Bay because we weren't getting capital for investment and our facilities were rapidly deteriorating. I was vice president at the time and all the senior managers were in favour of it because the Hudson's Bay Company was so loaded up with debt from purchasing Zellers, Simpson's, K Mart and others. We were a very profitable part of the Hudson's Bay Company and I knew we would do very well under the new owners."*

*So-called civilization has brought many dubious benefits to the north. Drugs and crime are a blight on some communities that were entirely free of these problems when Coles began his career. Does he feel that the overall impact of modernity has been negative or positive? "Oh it's definitely changed for the better," he says. "The fur business has collapsed, and the native people and the Inuit couldn't make a living off the land like they did years ago. When I started, the hospital ship would come once a year. Out in the hunting camps, if people got seriously ill they just died. If a plane was arriving in the wintertime we'd have to soak rolls of toilet paper in kerosene and put them in coffee cans and light them on fire to mark the runway. Now we have 737 jet airliners landing at nice little airports where the local people have good jobs grading the runways, maintaining the aircraft, running the transportation systems and so on. And they still live in their home communities so they can hunt and fish and camp out on the land and enjoy that beautiful country. So in many ways these people in the north now have the best of both worlds."*

Only adventurous souls would experience the brute and beauty of the Arctic. ABOVE: Don Coles operating the company radio system, "the only communication system with the outside world." OPPOSITE, LEFT TO RIGHT: Coles sporting a caribou parka and sheepskin boots; travelling by dog team; in the 1960s, Coles' responsibilities also included buying fur.

Derek Riley says that Trott, for one thing, promised to introduce inventory control technology, which would likely save the company a lot of money. "Canadian Tire's approach to inventory control was much superior to that of The Bay," Riley says. "Computers were still foreign to the way that the northern stores did business. It was Trott's belief that if goods aren't needed, they shouldn't be in the warehouse, piling up interest, and on this account alone he promised to save us needless expenses."

As Jim Oborne recalls, "Ralph seemed to be a very hard-charging guy who didn't really have a lot of respect for the old way of doing things. He promised a different management style, and as a board, we believed that would be good for us."

In late 1989, Northern Stores sent Trott a job offer, and he accepted. "I had spent 15 years at Canadian Tire and was ready for a change. And I liked the kind of challenge that Northern Stores was facing."

Trott remembers that the job started off on a positive note. "On my first day I arrived at 8:00 in the morning and Derek Riley, who was the chairman of the board at the time, was sitting in the president's office behind the desk, and I walked in and said, 'Hi, I'm Ralph, and you remember me? I'm here to start work today.'

"Derek immediately got up and walked around the desk, and said, 'You sit in the president's chair, Ralph, that's your chair. I'm glad you're here. It's your company. I only want one thing from you. And that is to build a great Canadian company.'

"With that, Derek walked out the door, saying. 'I'll see you at the next board meeting.'"

Trott says that showed him he was "aligned with the right chairman who put a lot of faith in me." He then walked around to introduce himself to the staff. "There were eight or nine vice presidents and none of them had met me yet. I approached each one and said, 'Hi, I'm Ralph Trott. I'm here to build a great Canadian company. So what do you do?'"

## SHAKING THINGS UP

Trott says he was "a change catalyst" at the venerable company. "My job was to shake things up. To make a bit of a statement about the kinds of changes that were about to take place, I had the old entrance door removed and new lighting installed in the hallway. Instantly the place felt more accessible to everybody; they could see what was going on."

Trott says Canadian Tire was a very competitive retail environment where employees had to "earn their stripes" on a day-to-day basis. "Nobody cared what happened last week, let alone a century ago. At Northern Stores Inc. there had been no reinvestment in systems, in real estate, in distribution facilities, in people or in training. Some of the senior people were very good, but some of them weren't going to fit in with the new order, so I let them go. They couldn't have worked for me anyway. I had one vice president who, from the moment I joined the company, went on sick leave and was gone for three months. Eventually he came in to say, 'I can't work for you. You're too young. You've got long hair, you're a hippy.' But there were other guys who were good, and they stayed."

Don Coles says that Trott's arrival at the company clearly marked the end of one era and the beginning of another. "From the moment Ralph walked in the door everything changed. Many of the people with 20 or 30 years of employment with The Bay were uncomfortable with him. They liked the old way of doing things and they didn't see the need for change. For example, some of them didn't use computers and objected to abandoning the old system of manual recordkeeping. Well, Ralph was very aggressive about modernizing and that was a real shock to the system. But it was a shock we needed."

Coles says Trott didn't just set out to change the way the company did business; he turned the place upside down. "The HBC was a top-down system," Coles explains. "We were told what to

**MARCH 1993**
Edward Kennedy appointed Executive VP and COO; becomes Chair of Alaskan subsidiary.

**APRIL 1993**
NWC opens $12.2-million Winnipeg Logistics Service Centre, which combines soft goods and hard goods distribution capability with automated systems, and merchandise picking and handling equipment designed for small quantities.

MY JOB WAS TO SHAKE THINGS UP. TO MAKE A BIT OF A STATEMENT ABOUT THE KINDS OF CHANGES THAT WERE ABOUT TO TAKE PLACE. I HAD AN OLD ENTRANCE DOOR REMOVED AND NEW LIGHTING INSTALLED IN THE HALLWAY. INSTANTLY THE PLACE FELT MORE ACCESSIBLE TO EVERYBODY; THEY COULD SEE WHAT WAS GOING ON.

do, and we followed those orders with no questions asked. Ralph introduced the 'bottom-up' model, in which each employee was given a lot of responsibility and a considerable workload. He had a lot of respect for his staff and he really listened. He worked very, very hard and expected the same from his troops. A couple of years after he took over, I was put in charge of changing the company's distribution system, bringing our distribution centres home to Winnipeg, and it was a rough time for all of us. I've never worked so hard in my life. I wasn't too happy about it and my wife wasn't too happy about it either. But Ralph sent her a large bouquet of flowers to show her he understood the sacrifices we were all making. That's what he was like. He expected a lot from you, but he never expected you to do what he wasn't doing himself."

Trott was always on the hunt for sharp, aggressive young people to help him rebuild the company, and in the autumn of 1989, he met someone who would become an important ally. "My phone rang one day and I grabbed it on the first ring — that was my style, something we did at Canadian Tire. This fellow on the line told me he was an investment banker and was interested in chatting with me. Winnipeg is a small pond, and the word had got out fairly quickly that I was a new president. He said, 'would you mind having lunch with me?' So, I said sure, I'll meet you for lunch. His name was Edward Kennedy."

## THE KID FROM THE PAS

Back in the 1970s The Hudson's Bay Company opened a new junior department store in The Pas, Manitoba, and within days, a local kid named Edward Kennedy made his way with the rest of the town to see this new store with "carpet on the floors and the latest city clothing styles." An old community with roots in the fur trade, The Pas had a legendary reputation of being a sort of northern version of Deadwood. The local bars thronged with loggers and millworkers, and every year, at the midwinter Trappers' Festival, tough woodsmen showed off their prowess by skinning muskrats and carrying 800 pounds of flour on their backs. It was a curious place to sell fashion. But the north was changing. The new motto of the province of Manitoba was "Growing to beat 70" and The Bay was aggressively expanding across rural Canada, riding a resource-fueled boom that seemed to have no limits.

The six Kennedy kids were members of the town's business class. Their father operated a fuel dealership and made enough money to send each of them south to school. Edward Kennedy says, "We spent lots of time outdoors because we only had one TV channel and the programs were a week late. We played every sport that existed and a few that were unique to The Pas, like a version of hide and seek with 20 on each team and a 'playing field' that was half backyard and half bush. I liked The Pas a lot. But my

NOVEMBER 1993
First AC Tomorrow Store opens
in St. Mary's, Alaska.

1994
The Business Innovation Project (BIP) is launched
to help redesign NWC's Canadian supply chain.

>>

parents stressed education and social responsibility. There was always an understanding that if we were to achieve our potential, we might have to move away."

So they moved. One of his sisters became a doctor and another became a lawyer. A younger brother went on to run the family's growing fuel business, and another — Gerard Kennedy — recently ran for the leadership of the federal Liberal party. (Some political analysts argue that he would be prime minister today if the party had chosen him over Michael Ignatieff.) Edward was the oldest boy, and at the age of 14 he went off to boarding school, first St. John's Ravenscourt in Winnipeg, then Ivey in London and Osgoode Hall in Toronto. With both business and law degrees under his belt, he worked for a few years in Toronto before landing a job in Winnipeg as an investment banker.

Like Jim Oborne, Kennedy faced some raised eyebrows on his decision to move back to Manitoba. "I worked on the 36th floor of the TD Bank tower in Toronto. It was a 100-person law firm and it was filled with young men and women from small towns like The Pas who had worked their butts off to get to Bay Street. So when I told one of the senior partners and my mentor, Jack Geller, that I was leaving the firm after only one year, he almost fell off his chair. He asked me what on earth I was going to do — meaning what could possibly be better than this — and I said I was going to become an investment banker. He straightened up again and seemed relieved that at least I had picked another profession that was part of the Toronto business establishment. Then I told him I was moving to Winnipeg. His jaw dropped again. All he said was, 'Well I guess you have to start somewhere. Good luck.'"

For Kennedy the move to Winnipeg was more than a move away from law. "A good education was respected within our family," he says. "But the privileges that came with the package were not. You were expected to make your own way, based on merit. For me, moving away from the business centre of Canada was a step towards real success, not a step away."

So he moved to Winnipeg and began working as an investment

Edward Kennedy (above) joined The North West Company in 1989. OPPOSITE: The annual Trappers' Festival in The Pas, Manitoba, celebrates the portages of historic cross-country journeys with a flour-packing contest.

48

banker at Pemberton Securities. On that autumn day in 1989 when he went for lunch with Ralph Trott, they met at Dubrovnik's, a stylish old restaurant on the leafy banks of the Assiniboine River. It was an interesting pairing: both men were young, ambitious and intense. (Kennedy, 31, was a competitive hockey and soccer player and Trott, 39, drove race cars for a hobby.) "I didn't call Ralph because I was looking for a job," says Kennedy. "I knew that the Northern Stores Inc. was going to be a publicly traded company so I called Ralph to see if my firm could help. But Ralph was a captivating guy and I would've enjoyed meeting him for lunch anyways."

Trott says the lunch conversations were just as interesting for him. "I was intrigued with the fact that Edward grew up in The Pas, which was obviously our market. In our business you have to analyze your customer and find out what they want. But I had no knowledge of the north whatsoever. I needed someone who knew how to ask the right questions."

"Ralph was looking for the best way to apply his retailing savvy to this chain of northern stores," says Kennedy. "He was faced with northern logistics, the weather and the culture of the aboriginal communities. He was interested when I pointed out that you can't try to sell sixes of an individual dress, for example, because it's a small town and Sally doesn't want to be wearing the same style and colour as Mary. You have to spend extra time in the warehouse sorting the clothes and making sure there's a lot of variety."

They also talked about price and quality. "For outdoor living," says Kennedy, "clothing and equipment has to be top quality, because the conditions are extreme and people's lives depend on it. Price comes second. I'm sure he heard the same things from his senior team but maybe it impressed him coming from an outsider like me."

They met for lunch several times, and the conversations focused mainly on Trott's challenge — to modernize the company without losing its traditional market. "We talked about the

**1994**
AC Express outlets launched; first Burger King opened in Dutch Harbor.

**1994**
Northern Pharmacy (Ontario) Inc. opens first outlet in store in Moosonee, Ontario.

CROSSING PATHS WITH EDWARD WAS GOOD FORTUNE;
HE HAD ALL OF THE CREDENTIALS I WAS LOOKING FOR IN
A BUSINESS DEVELOPMENT PERSON. HE WAS ALSO SOMEONE
WHO WAS YOUNG, AGGRESSIVE AND KEEN, HAD GOOD
PEOPLE SKILLS, GREAT INTELLECTUAL CAPABILITY AND AN
ENGAGING STYLE.

company as though it were a venerable clock on a mantelpiece," says Kennedy. "Like the clock, the northern stores had ticked away for years, keeping good time. But there was a fragility to the way it worked — if you took it apart you might lose or break a critical piece and ruin the whole enterprise."

Trott began to feel that Kennedy would be a good addition to his corporate team. "Edward had grown up in a small northern town. He'd had the exposure to native culture. He knew a lot about the community. Some things just fall into place when you're lucky. Crossing paths with Edward was good fortune; he had all of the credentials I was looking for in a business development person. He was also someone who was young, aggressive and keen, had good people skills, great intellectual capability and an engaging style."

Kennedy says that during one of their lunches Trott popped the question. "At some point Ralph said, 'Why don't you come and work for us?' The fact that the board had hired him showed that they were ready to make some bold moves. Ralph wasn't specific about what I might do in this new job but said they never had anyone do corporate development. So that was the first idea, and I joined the company in December 1989."

## STEPPING FORWARD

Earl Boon recalls that Edward Kennedy's arrival marked another step forward for the company. "The company was rapidly transforming, and Ralph decided we needed a new emblem. It was to symbolize the company's bright future. He felt that 'Perseverance' sounded like someone hanging on by their nails. He said he didn't think it was appropriate for a company going forward. The board agreed, and I can't say I disagreed. He said to me, 'Look, you've got to come up with something else.'"

There are different versions of what happened next. Boon recalls plunging into the library and working his way through hundreds of ideas and words and concepts. He wasn't just looking for a corporate logo, he was looking for a word that would both evoke the can-do attitude of pioneering Nor'westers like Alexander Mackenzie and David Thompson, and symbolize the wide-open entrepreneurial spirit of a company gearing up for the 21st century. "I finally chose the word 'Enterprising,'" says Boon. "I took it to Ralph and he said, 'Yes, that's it.'"

Ralph Trott says he can't recall the exact details. "I thought I was the one who came up with the word 'Enterprising' but if Earl Boon says he came up with it, I won't argue with him."

Edward Kennedy impressed Ralph Trott with his intimate knowledge of customers' needs. Kennedy insisted on offering top-quality clothing and equipment for extreme weather conditions.

**51**

>>

**52**

Ian Sutherland says the board and the management also felt that the company needed a new name. "We were still called Northern Stores Inc., and the outlets still wore their "Hudson's Bay Northern Stores" signage. So it was clear that it was time for a change, but selecting a new name can be surprisingly difficult."

Jim Oborne says, "the board members wanted to rename it The Northwest Company. It was poetic justice, because the stores had never gotten much respect and had always served as a cash cow for The Bay and now here they were, reborn under the banner of The Bay's old rival. And the Northwest Company was always a distinct entity within The Bay anyway."

Derek Riley recalls that "Imperial Oil and the Province of Ontario owned the rights to the name. But when we told them we wanted to revive the old enterprise, they gave us the rights to the name with their blessing. We spelled the name differently, to reflect the new era — it became The North West Company."

## MAPPING THE FUTURE

One of Ralph Trott's first tasks was to map out where the company needed to go over the next five years. He called this plan "Enterprise 95." It grew into a thorough size-up of what lay ahead for North West and it generated some controversy.

Kennedy says that he was hired with no clear job description. One of his responsibilities was "legal counsel" but he wasn't licensed to practice in Manitoba and had only a year of actual lawyering under his belt. What he really wanted to do was help build the business, and very soon after he joined the firm, Trott put him in a leadership role on Enterprise 95. Kennedy says that as the plan developed, there was "pushback" from the veterans in the company. "In any long-established business there is tension between old and new. Enterprise 95 clearly showed that tradition wasn't going to win the fight against direct-order shopping and the big-box stores that appealed to northerners on their

**1995**
Earl Boon, VP of Corporate Planning and Diversified Business, retires after 41 years with NWC.

**1995**
Healthy Food Choices program launched. NWC's in-house nutritional plan ensures the availability of healthy foods in stores, and includes community education and informative labeling system.

"power shopping" trips to the city. To win there had to be hard commitments to the future. And that afflicted the comfort level of some people."

Kennedy points out that the company's veteran managers were "incredibly resourceful," but they had never been asked to plan out more than a year or two. Enterprise 95 was a picture of how the company would position itself for the next five years and beyond. "We asked: What kind of values do we want to work by? Where will our growth come from? Should we keep or sell certain stores? What about joint ventures with First Nations? What will the training program look like? All these things were considered, and it was stimulating activity. Through the whole process we didn't disparage our past or the contributions of our long-serving people — instead, we shifted the emphasis to the present and the

future and called it 'Making History Today.'"

Ian Sutherland recalls that one of the most difficult exercises in Enterprise 95 was deciding whether to move towards urban centres or stick with stores in remote communities. "At the time, we had both," he says. "Some of the larger stores were 30,000- to 60,000-foot outlets that looked more like a Zellers than a northern store. Running one of these was a far cry from managing a little store in a community of 700 people. Still, the larger stores were popular with some of the board members because they gave us good visibility in these growing towns."

Jim Oborne comments that sticking with the big stores would have had serious financial implications. "It would have required investing even more of our cash flow away from the core business and probably cutting the dividend. And that would have been an

1995
Learning from the successes and setbacks of Enterprise 95, NWC launches Enterprise 98, a strategic action plan that aggressively builds on the company's market dominance in northern Canada.

>>

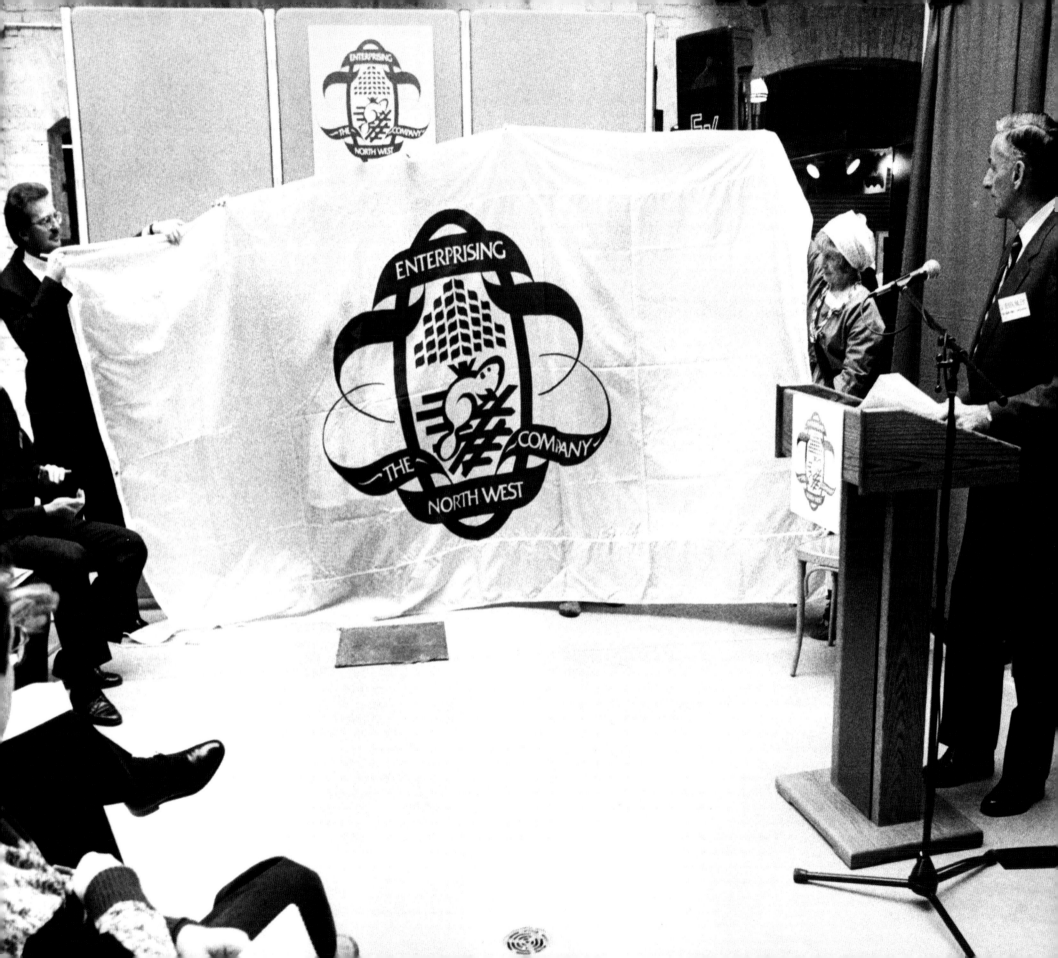

HE WASN'T JUST LOOKING FOR A CORPORATE LOGO, HE WAS LOOKING FOR A WORD THAT WOULD BOTH EVOKE THE CAN-DO ATTITUDE OF PIONEERING NOR'WESTERS LIKE ALEXANDER MACKENZIE AND DAVID THOMPSON, AND SYMBOLIZE THE WIDE-OPEN ENTREPRENEURIAL SPIRIT OF A COMPANY GEARING UP FOR THE 21ST CENTURY.

WE COMMITTED TO THE TRUE NORTHERN STORES. WE COMMITTED TO BUILDING OUR EXPERTISE AND COMMUNITY PARTNERSHIPS WITH A SHARED APPROACH TO GROWTH AND SUCCESS. FOR OUR CUSTOMERS, ENTERPRISE 95 MEANT BETTER STORES, NEW SERVICES, COMPUTERIZED CHECKOUTS AND FOR US, A SIMPLE PRINCIPLE TO WORK BY — "CUSTOMER SERVICE IS OUR FIRST PRIORITY."

56

unpopular move with many of our employee shareholders and founder investors, because they had their life savings on the line."

Trott bundled up his evidence, went into the next board meeting and broke the news. "I told them, 'I want to get rid of the junior department stores.' Well, that was not something they wanted to hear. We argued about it for quite a while, then Derek Riley, who is just a super gentleman, said, 'Is this how you want to proceed as President?' I said, 'It's the only way I will proceed.' He told me to leave them alone while they talked it over. I left the room and looked at Edward and more or less said, 'Well, I guess we're going to find out very quickly whether we still have jobs or not.' Then after about an hour they called me back in and said 'okay, you can sell the department stores.'"

Enterprise 95 didn't just define what the company wouldn't do (e.g., no more expansion into the department store market) it also helped define what the North West Company would do. As Kennedy explains, "We committed to the true northern stores. We committed to building our expertise and community partnerships with a shared approach to growth and success. For our customers, Enterprise 95 meant better stores, new services and computerized checkouts, and for us, a simple principle to work by — 'Customer Service is Our First Priority.'

## A BOLD REMAKE

In order to make Enterprise 95 a success it was necessary to win over the company's front line managers — the people who ran the stores. "These fellows are the public face of the company," says Derek Riley. "Some of them were old Bay men who were accustomed to doing things their own way. They had complete independence throughout the year except when their supervisor arrived for inspection and then they lived in fear. But most of the time nobody knew what they were doing. Now they had to buy in to the spirit of the plan or it wouldn't work."

Says Trott, "I went up north to meet the store managers and explain what we wanted to do. My style is informal. I'd insist they call me by my first name, no more of this 'mister and sir' stuff. When I asked them what they thought was wrong with the business they thought it was a trick question. But I encouraged them, and gradually they relaxed and started speaking their minds. We put their comments on video, and distributed the tapes across the country."

Shifting entrenched store practices and standards was a daunting task made even more complex by the incredibly wide geography of the company's store network. Trott says that they adopted a 'rifle strategy' as opposed to the shotgun approach.

---

**MARCH 1995**
Edward Kennedy moves to Anchorage, Alaska, to become CEO of Alaska Commercial.

**1996**
Quickstop grows to 37 locations. The stores achieve $15 million in sales in three years.

The first Quickstop convenience store in Ashern, MB, offered a Pizza Hut, KFC, petroleum products and automotive supplies, as well as video rentals, 1994.

"Our idea was to take one geographic section of the country and do it right. Let's say there were 10 zones. We would take 1 zone and rebuild the thing — put in the right district manager, the right store manager, invest in the facilities, put in the point of sales systems, fix everything in that zone. Then we rolled that out to the next zone."

It was an expensive and time-consuming strategy, and it required a leap of faith for people to trust that they weren't just tinkering with the old cuckoo clock, but were building a brand new mechanism that would last. The 1990s were bringing in rapid technological and social changes and the ground was moving underfoot. On the micro level, innovations like the cellular phone and the fax machine changed the way people conducted business every day. These might have seemed like cosmetic changes but they weren't — during that decade, for example, the number of self-employed people working out of home offices in Canada increased tenfold and this new connectivity meant the company's markets were, at least virtually, less and less remote.

Jim Oborne adds "The North West Company could not have picked a more unpredictable time to be plunging into new

1996
NWC receives Government of Canada Healthy Environment Award for development of Environmental Management System and Petroleum Products Handling training programs.

1996
People First program begins. The employee-centred initiative invests time on education and development programs for all NWC associates.

ventures. The early 1990s were a time of very rough sledding. The global economy was in turmoil. The market was skittish, and retailers like us were facing high interest rates and some of the lowest spending figures in Canadian history. But Ralph and Edward made real progress in that difficult environment. Ralph promised to transform the company, and there's no question that he was succeeding."

Ralph Trott says there were definite signs that his bold remake of the company was paying off. "We had good financial success in the years '91, '92 and '93, and we were very successful in our taking the company public and other initiatives like signing up with Pizza Hut and KFC."

He notes that one of his proudest moments at The North West Company had nothing to do with increasing sales or improvements to the company's bottom line. It had to with the growing happiness and confidence of his staff. "I was at some social event and Don Coles' secretary came up to me and said that our company now had the largest number of members at Toastmasters in Winnipeg. And it was because more and more people were feeling the freedom to stand up and speak out. We were turning into this very vibrant culture where everybody was offering up ideas. The word was getting out — The North West Company is a cool place, and the young people in the city wanted to come and work for us."

## BUILDING ON ENTERPRISE 95

"Then, just as thing were going well, we got some bad news," says Jim Oborne. "Ralph told us he was leaving the company."

As Trott explains, "My oldest son, Jeffrey, was a national competitive figure skater. But he had moved to Ontario to complete his training. So he was 15 and living in Ontario and my wife was having a heart attack about that. My son wasn't enjoying his time in Ontario by himself either and around the same time Molson called me and asked if I'd entertain the prospect of fixing Ontario-based Beaver Lumber. I didn't give

that much thought, but then I started to think such an offer was possibly the answer. It would fix my personal issues and put my family unit back together. So I started to consider moving on. I believed my journey at North West was complete anyway. Someone needed to follow me now, and take this good company and make it perfect."

"We said goodbye to Ralph on good terms," says Jim Oborne. "But it shocked all of us. Once again we were left with no CEO. We felt that Edward was too young and inexperienced for the job, so we asked Ian Sutherland to step in and appointed Edward as the Chief Operating Officer."

Sutherland had significant business interests in Toronto, but he agreed to move to Winnipeg and become CEO. As Ralph Trott departed the President's office, he agreed that Sutherland was a good choice. "There are times when a company needs a change leader and times when it needs a strong manager. I was good at change, in the sense that I knew how to create a new culture in the workplace and fire up the troops, but once that new culture was established I wasn't particularly good at day-to-day management. Upon my departure the company needed someone like Ian Sutherland."

Sutherland says he looked forward to returning to Winnipeg and running the company. "I'm a Winnipegger at heart so that appealed to me, and I had some ideas for the company I wanted to pursue as President."

Under Sutherland's direction the company became even more focused on being a successful community retailer. One indicator was the presence of local residents within each store's management team. "Ian supported the First Nation store leases that Len Flett and I were working on," says Edward Kennedy. "He also saw the need to develop and promote more community members into supervisory and management positions, especially within the aboriginal markets that we served. Ian demanded compensation practices that would attract the best local candidates including many that were already working for us. He set hard targets and it

**1996**
First National Bank of Anchorage installs ATMs in 17 Alaska Commercial stores.

**DECEMBER 1996**
Jerry Bittner appointed CEO of Alaska Commercial.

>>

WE WERE TURNING INTO THIS VERY VIBRANT CULTURE WHERE EVERYBODY WAS OFFERING UP IDEAS. THE WORD WAS GETTING OUT — THE NORTH WEST COMPANY IS A COOL PLACE, AND THE YOUNG PEOPLE IN THE CITY WANTED TO COME AND WORK FOR US.

After accepting the position of president, Ian Sutherland told the *Winnipeg Free Press*, "It's a bit scary. You have the ultimate responsibility. There's a risk there and it's not an insignificant risk to deal with."

worked. We moved from 50 aboriginal supervisors and managers to over 200 within three years. No other organization in Canada had achieved this before and it was a great feeling to hear Ian publicly report our progress at the annual shareholder meetings."

Sutherland completed Enterprise 95 and then re-energized it as a tighter three-year plan called E 98 with a renewed commitment to the "details" of training, store investment and new product and service growth, all while working on making the company's new Alaska venture viable. It was a heavy agenda but still left room for the company to consider other innovations.

Says Sutherland, "One of the things that had been weighing on my mind for a good long while was our taxation status. Two of our major owners were the Saskatchewan Government Pension Fund and the Manitoba Teachers Pension Fund. In fact over half of our ownership was tax-deferred pension plans like these as well as individual RRSPs. We became concerned that, with corporate tax rates at about 45 percent, the returns to these owners was being substantially reduced by tax. For example, a 10 percent pre-tax return on equity would be 10 percent if the funds received the income directly but only 5.5 percent if The North West Company had to pay corporate tax first."

Sutherland discussed this dilemma with David Broadhurst, a long-time tax advisor to the company and future board member,

devising different scenarios and structures that might reduce this impact on non-taxable shareholders. "We looked at structures where the funds would hold convertible or participating company debt. These structures made NWC appear overleveraged with too much debt and the Board concluded that the risk to the enterprise would be elevated."

Some oil and gas companies had begun creating trusts that would flow their income before tax to the owners who were trust unit holders instead of shareholders. "David and I thought that this could be applied to The North West Company by converting the shares of NWC into units of a trust. The trust distributions would be deductible for tax purposes for NWC, allowing almost double the previous dividend at the same cost to the Company."

Sutherland then went to work to convince the major shareholders that this would improve their returns. "Because of the novelty of the concept, they were initially skeptical but in the end, supportive," he says. "The banks understood the concept quickly and agreed. The bond holders took more time but eventually came onside. In June 1997 NWC officially became The North West Company Fund (NWF), the first company in Canada to convert to this structure without the sale of the company or a significant unit issue. The existing shareholders received one unit for each share held previously."

**DECEMBER 1996**
NWC creates national Aboriginal Relations Council, composed of aboriginal leaders from across Canada, including board member Len Flett.

**1997**
NWC celebrates 10 years as an independent company from HBC.

Previously, as a small- to mid-sized public company, NWC had difficulty establishing what it considered to be a full, fair price for its shares. After conversion to an income trust, NWF had a whole new set of analysts, funds and investors who liked the higher yield and eventually awarded NWF with a healthy valuation. Later, as NWF demonstrated above-average growth in profitability, the investment performance excelled further and became one of the top total return (yield plus growth) income trusts on the Toronto Stock Exchange. When Jim Flaherty ended the benefits of income trusts on Halloween 2007, North West decided to convert back to a taxable company. "NWC units slipped a bit on the bad tax news," says Sutherland. "But loyal owners stood fast, and investor analysts continued to give the company a premium rating."

**1997**
Northern Pharmacy starts distributing pharmaceuticals to nursing stations in Attawapiskat, Ontario.

**1997**
NWC becomes first non-resource company to change from a share corporation to an income trust.

>>

### CHAPTER THREE

# WEST TO ALASKA

WHEN PEOPLE SEE THAT YOU'RE HONEST, WELL-INTENTIONED AND TRYING TO GIVE THEM THE BEST GOODS AND SERVICES YOU CAN DELIVER, THEY WELCOME YOU AND START INVITING YOU TO PARTIES AND OTHER SOCIAL EVENTS.

In 1984 a young man named Rex Wilhelm graduated with an MBA from Washington State University and went looking for a job. It wasn't a good time for a married father of two to be unemployed. Interest rates were in the double digits. Inflation was on the rise. Gasoline prices had soared from 90 cents a gallon to $1.50, and the Jimmy Carter administration was fighting the recession by tightening up the money supply and advising people to save dollars they didn't have.

Wilhelm canvassed the job market and heard about a company called Alaska Commercial. "They operated a chain of retail stores across remote Alaska," he says. "But their headquarters were in Washington, so I went to see them. They offered me a job working in the store in Nome. It was a long way from the garden climate of Washington, but my wife and I figured that we would go up there, work hard for five years, save a pile of money and return to civilization once the recession was over."

They got rid of everything they owned, including their house and their dog ("Man, I hated parting with that dog") and climbed onto a plane headed north. "It was March, and when we landed in Nome it was pitch dark and 30 below zero. They put us up in this terrible, shabby little house and as soon as we walked in the door I looked at my wife and said, 'Honey, if we'd known it was going to be like this I don't think we ever would've left Washington.'"

The next day Wilhelm rose in the early morning darkness, put on a white shirt and a tie, and went off to see the retail store where he'd be applying his skills as a Master of Business Administration. "The store was a rather dumpy-looking old building on the edge of the Bering Sea. It was a bleak morning — snow drifting in off the sea ice and miserably cold. The manager met me at the door and told me that I'd better go home and put on some grubbier clothes. 'No one will trust you in that necktie.' But before I left he opened the door and turned on the lights. The floor seemed to be moving. It took a while for me to realize what I was looking at — the store was seething with rats."

**1997**
NWC acquires Crescent Multi-Foods.

**1997**
NWC receives Manitoba Round Table on the Environment and Economy Award of Excellence for its Petroleum Products Handling Training Program.

The building was like the stage setting for a 19th-century frontier movie — rough floors, shelves made of wooden planks and four cash registers of four different makes. But Wilhelm was determined to make the best of the situation. "We brought in some rat terriers and set them loose in the building. It was quite something to see them work. They'll grab a rat, give it a shake, toss it over their shoulder and dash after another one. They are very impressive dogs."

In short order the store was free of rodents, but the business was plagued with chronic problems. The pipes were always freezing. The heating system was inadequate. The building was falling apart. "Our owner was the Community Economic Development Corporation of Alaska, which comprised about 120 different native organizations. Their whole intent was to provide service at the lowest cost possible — profit was a dirty word. The trouble was they didn't build in any margin that could be reinvested in the business."

Catching fish in the Nome River before the workday starts May/ June 1984.

**MARCH 21, 1997**
Iain Ronald retires as Chairman
of the Board of Directors.

**MARCH 21, 1997**
Ian Sutherland appointed new
Chairman of the Board of Directors.

>>

**66**

Meanwhile he faced the almost comical adversity of life in the Arctic. When the school bus arrived in the morning, he or his wife would escort the kids out to the vehicle. "We were warned not to let the kids go outside and wait for the bus themselves. So we walked them out to the driver, who stood guard by the door of the bus with a shotgun. When we asked why he was carrying a gun, he explained about the polar bears that occasionally wander into town."

Despite the challenges, Wilhelm enjoyed working at the store. The local people were friendly and welcoming, especially after it became apparent that he and his wife intended to tough it out and stay. "When people see that you're honest, well-intentioned and trying to give them the best goods and services you can

deliver, they welcome you and start inviting you to parties and other social events."

Spring arrived, the barren lands sprouted flowers and Wilhelm and his wife began to feel better about their decision to move to Nome. "We actually began to enjoy it," he says. "But the problems at the company didn't go away. Alaska Commercial was trying to give the best deal to native people. But, ironically, they just ended up hurting their customers because they couldn't provide the level of service that people deserved. What the company needed was a new owner who would whip it into shape and run it properly."

As Wilhelm was starting to move up through the ranks of Alaska Commercial, his adopted state was beginning to attract the attention of the Ralph Trott-led team at the newly named

**MARCH 21, 1997**
Edward Kennedy returns to Winnipeg
and assumes position of President and
CEO of NWC.

**1998**
NWC celebrates its 15th anniversary and publishes
*The North West Company Frontier Merchants*, written
by Florida Town.

North West Company. (Trott was still CEO when Alaska came onto the radar screen.) After all, Enterprise 95 was about more than updating and solidifying the company's northern Canada business; it also had an eye to new markets. Edward Kennedy, Trott and the rest of the senior team promoted expanding geographically west instead of south.

Alaska presented an interesting opportunity. It was on the same latitude and shared many similarities with the markets that the company already served. "We knew how to operate stores in remote communities," says Kennedy. "And it looked like there was a lot of room for improvement in how retailing was being done in rural Alaska. On several occasions going back to the late '80s, senior people from our company went up to Alaska to assess the potential. Alaska Commercial was the largest retailer there. It was limping along, but to us it held that potential."

The Nor'westers split up into teams and visited every store in the Alaska Commercial network. "We asked our team to describe the store and the community. How were the customers, products, stores and their staff similar and different from northern Canada?"

## HERE COME THE CANADIANS

By now it was 1991, and Rex Wilhelm was based in Anchorage as a senior merchant. He had decided that he loved Alaska and was comfortably settled in with his family. He was one of the people the Nor'westers visited. "I was told by head office that these Canadians would be coming," says Wilhelm. "My bosses said to be nice to them, get them a cup of coffee, but keep your cards close and don't tell them anything."

Soon the moccasin telegraph was humming with the news that a Canadian company was thinking about buying Alaska Commercial. Controversy erupted in the local newspapers. "There was no question that the North West group had a number of strikes against them," says Wilhelm. "They were non-aboriginal, they were non-Alaskan and, heck, they weren't even American. But from the moment I met them, I felt hopeful that a deal would come together. They were hard-working, entrepreneurial guys with a serious commitment to the north. Sure, they were Canadian, but there's a lot of similarity between the Canadian north and Alaska, and they talked about spending money to bring our stores up to standard. That's exactly what we needed."

**1998**
NWC receives Conference Board of Canada Top Employer of Youth Best Practice Award.

**1998**
NWC food mix refined to target core shoppers with launch of "Best Value" — opening price and "Big Deals" programs.

# WHAT MAKES AN IDEAL STORE MANAGER?

*Establishing a stable, dedicated team of managers is a challenge for any retailer, and it is especially important when your stores are scattered across thousands of miles of remote Arctic wilderness. Mark Melton has managed stores for Alaska Commercial for 30 years — even before its acquisition by The North West Company — and he has some strong opinions about the sort of person who is best suited for a life in the north.*

*"First of all you have to be a hard worker," he says. "It's not the sort of job where you're putting in a fixed number of hours and then going home to your other life. At busy times of the year, the role of store manager takes up most of your waking hours, seven days a week."*

*Melton managed a variety of stores across rural Alaska and learned to cope with a spectacular array of hardships, not the least of which was the weather. "The coldest I've experienced was 72 below zero. And I'm not talking wind chill. That was an honest 72 below. It was so cold once that none of the vehicles would start, so I walked to work. When I got to the store the pipes had all burst and there was water spraying everywhere. The produce had all frozen and the tomatoes were as hard as baseballs."*
*He says that the quality of infrastructure improved dramatically when The North West Company acquired Alaska Commercial's retail network. The NWC built many new stores and renovated others, but nothing could be done to improve the weather. "It's a long winter," he says. "It's dark for 20 hours a day and sometimes it's 40 below for weeks at a time. The air carriers won't fly when it's below minus 40, so we often have to cope with very limited supplies."*

*Melton adds that northerners have a tremendous sense of cooperation, and their good cheer and humour make the hardship easier. "You learn to see it as an adventure. For example, one time my kids came running into the house because a cow moose was chasing them. They had come upon the moose on the snowmobile trail out behind the house and she chased them off the machine and wouldn't let them anywhere near it. She and her calf stayed right around the thing for five days, pooped all over it and wouldn't let us get it back. Another time we stood at the window of our house watching an Alaskan brown bear tear our shed apart. If you live in Alaska I can guarantee that you'll never be bored."*

*As well as having a taste for hard work and adventure, the ideal northern store manager should have good social skills. "You have to be a people person," Melton says. "Life in the north is all about relationships. You have to be fair and honest. Customers are giving you their precious money, so there has to be a bond of trust. You have an important role in the community; like it or not, you are going to be placed on a bit of a pillar. People will have high expectations of your attitude and your behaviour. You're going to be a banker, a diplomat, a baseball coach and maybe even a bit of a therapist. And although you work hard and give a lot of yourself to your community, you get repaid many times over in friendship."*

*When Melton was diagnosed with life-threatening cancer in 1995 (likely caused by a pack-a-day smoking habit) he had to go to Portland, Oregon, for treatment. "The community support was unbelievable. Townspeople organized three parties and raised eight thousand dollars to help with my expenses. It was very moving, I'll tell you. When I recovered I began visiting schools to warn kids about the dangers of smoking."*

*He points out that each community is like a big extended family. "Everyone watches out for everybody. You leave your keys in your truck and you know it's safe; you never have to worry about where your kids are, someone is sure to have their eye on them."*

*He raised four children of his own, and says there's no shortage of fun and outdoor adventure. "The best time of my life was coaching basketball and baseball. One time, I promised the kids that if they won the championship they could cut my hair and do it in any style they wanted. Well, they won, and they gave me a reverse Mohawk. For weeks, my hairdo was the main subject of entertainment for people coming into the store."*

*Despite the rough weather, the difficulties of running a store in a remote location and the demands of the job, Melton has never regretted choosing a career in the north. "I never felt like I was missing anything. Actually it was the opposite. Once you've lived in the north, it's such a rich life that you never want to live anywhere else."*

THE NORTH WEST COMPANY BECAME THE PROUD OWNER OF 16 DILAPIDATED GENERAL STORES IN ALASKA, ACCESSIBLE ONLY BY AIR OR WATER. IT WAS A BOLD MOVE AND A CHALLENGE THAT WAS TRUE TO THE SPIRIT OF THE EARLIER NORTHWEST COMPANY — ONCE AGAIN IT WAS PLUNGING INTO COMPETITION WITH DEEPLY ENTRENCHED RIVALS IN A COUNTRY WHERE IT ARGUABLY DIDN'T BELONG.

Controversy was also building back in Winnipeg, where the board was divided over the wisdom of challenging the Americans on their own turf. Ian Sutherland recalls that one risk was the poor track record of other Canadian retailers in the American marketplace. "Some of our board members were very experienced merchants who thought we were making a serious mistake. The supporters believed we'd be different, because we were northerners, our operating conditions were quite similar to Alaska Commercial and we had extensive experience serving aboriginal communities. But the debate was heated."

Edward Kennedy says the controversy in Alaska came down to whether or not the deal would be good for native people. "That was a legitimate concern, and we had to convince the communities that they would benefit from our ownership. It was a political and drawn-out bureaucratic process that took countless trips to Alaska, and it went right down to the wire. At one point Ralph Trott sent out a notice to our employees that negotiations had fallen apart and that the project was dead."

Nonetheless, three months later, in the late autumn of 1992, the deal finally went through and The North West Company became the proud owner of 16 dilapidated general stores in rural Alaska, accessible only by air or water. It was a bold move and a challenge that was true to the spirit of the first Northwest Company — once again it was plunging into competition with deeply entrenched

rivals in a country where it arguably didn't belong. Alaska looked good on paper, but now they had to make it work. As Kennedy puts it, "We were the dog that caught the bus."

## MAKING ALASKA WORK

Now that The North West Company owned Alaska Commercial's stores, it entered a tunnel of anxiety that would be familiar to any homeowner. "It starts as an adventure," says Kennedy. "You see the house; you think the house has a great upside, so you buy it. Then the house needs a lot of work, and the money worries begin."

Board veteran Ian Sutherland says, "We made a few strategic mistakes initially. We built new stores in key communities, like Dutch Harbor and Nome, to defend against a wholesaler who had decided to become a retail competitor. In Dutch Harbor this competitor built a very expensive store that served the purpose of hurting us. Actually it hurt both of us because the community became over-stored. At the same time the town was shrinking because the fishing industry was going through a difficult cycle. We were killing each other out there on the Aleutian Islands."

Kennedy says there were other errors — like underestimating the difference between the Canadian and American consumer. "The U.S. retail goods market is much bigger and their consumers expect far more selection. They want to shop at any time of day or night. They want their soft drinks to be cold, even the cases. To

AC Value Center's roots can be traced back to 1776 when Catherine the Great granted trading rights to the Russian-American Trading Company. In 1867, when the U.S. bought Alaska, the company became Alaska Commercial Company. At the time of the purchase by NWC in 1992, Alaska Commercial had 16 retail locations.

**1998**
Launch of Vision 2000+, a three-year plan to grow "with and within" the North by investing in stores and offering new everyday products and services.

**1999**
Forty-eight Canadian locations reprofiled with expanded fresh- and frozen-food sections.

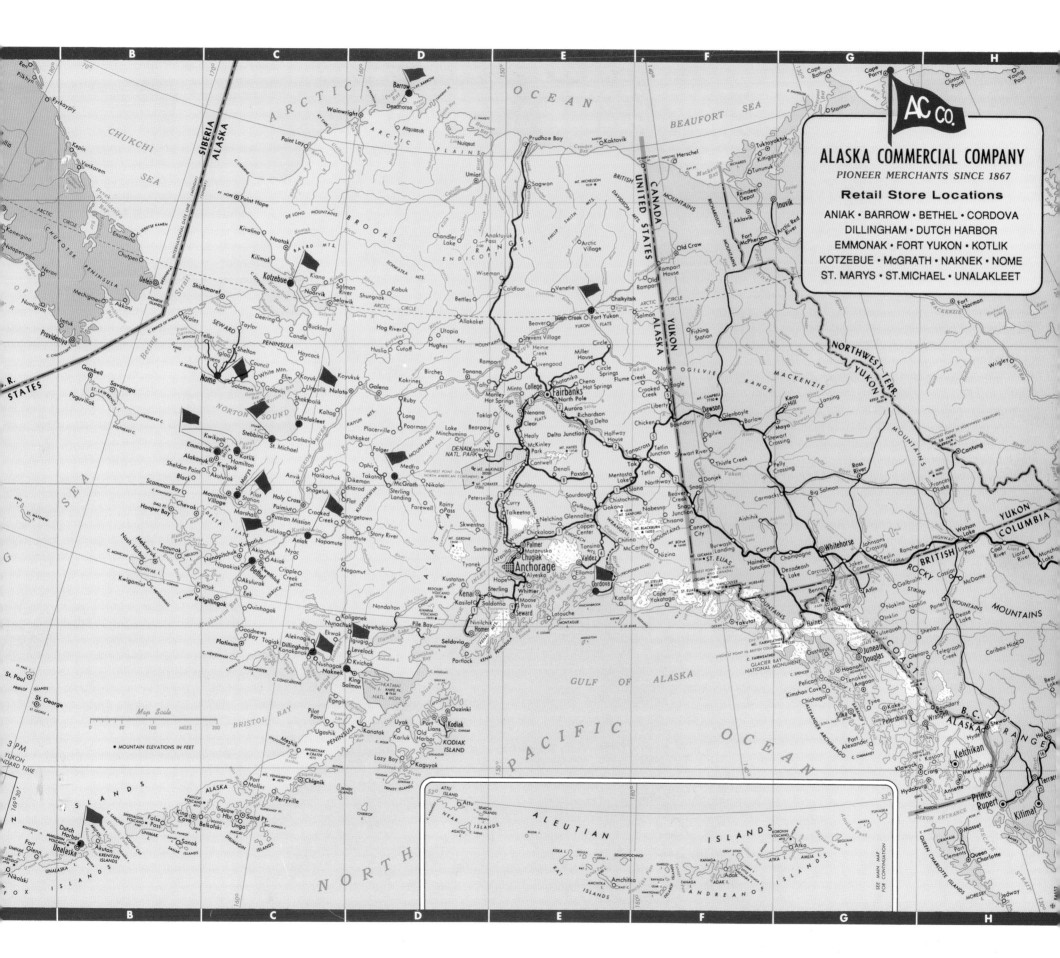

# ALASKA COMMERCIAL COMPANY
## PIONEER MERCHANTS SINCE 1867
### Retail Store Locations
ANIAK • BARROW • BETHEL • CORDOVA
DILLINGHAM • DUTCH HARBOR
EMMONAK • FORT YUKON • KOTLIK
KOTZEBUE • McGRATH • NAKNEK • NOME
ST. MARYS • ST. MICHAEL • UNALAKLEET

VERY SOON AFTER WE ACQUIRED ALASKA COMMERCIAL IT
BECAME APPARENT THAT WE HAD PROBLEMS. THE STORES WERE
LOSING MONEY, THE COMPETITION WAS INTENSIFYING AND SOME
OF THE BOARD MEMBERS WERE SAYING, "WHAT DID I TELL YOU?"

a Canadian merchant that's crazy. Cold individual drinks, yes. But why waste energy, especially expensive northern, diesel-power electricity, running coolers full of cases of pop? If you want cold drinks put them in the fridge when you get home. Well, that logic was worth 10 cents because all that counts is what your customer expects. We were learning that American shoppers, even northerners, wanted varieties of frozen pizza and guacamole and specialty items that you just don't see in small stores in Canada. We were building new facilities and spending millions of dollars, and still our Alaska stores weren't performing like our Canadian locations. It was clear that we had to address these issues, and we had to do it quickly."

In The North West Company boardroom and among its executives there was growing concern with the whole endeavour in Alaska. Under the ownership of the Hudson's Bay Company, the northern stores had always made money; during the troubled 1980s, the northern store network had even helped subsidize the various white-elephant department stores that the company was maintaining down south. Now the Canadian stores were supporting the money-losing stores of Alaska Commercial. It was déjà vu.

Sutherland says, "Very soon after we acquired Alaska Commercial it became apparent that we had problems. We had brought in a couple of executives to run the Alaska show and they weren't working out. The stores were losing money, the competition was intensifying and some of the board members were saying, 'What did I tell you?' We discussed all options,

including selling Alaska Commercial to our competitors. You should have seen the smiles on their faces when we approached them with cap in hand. They were willing to talk, of course, but they were only going to pay us a fraction of what we'd invested."

## SENDING "THE KID" TO FIX IT

Selling Alaska Commercial was a distasteful option, but things were getting serious. Derek Riley, the founding chairman, says many of the board members argued that the best guy to fix Alaska was one of the guys who suggested it in the first place. "Edward seemed like the obvious man to go up to Alaska," says Riley. "It was an opportunity to challenge him. Our thinking was, 'Let's send the kid up to Alaska and see what he can do. And if he works out, we'll make him CEO.'"

Ian Sutherland says Riley's suggestion resonated with most of the board. "When Ralph Trott left, both Edward and I were candidates for CEO, and Derek believed that it was in the best interest of the company to put us both in senior roles, myself as President and Edward as the Chief Operating Officer. When Alaska Commercial needed more hands-on attention, the thinking was that his experience would be augmented by an operating role as President and CEO in Alaska, combined with his board and executive role for the whole company. There was an expectation that, once the Alaska management team was strengthened and the operation turned around in three to five years, Edward would return to Canada."

The 1992 purchase of Alaska Commercial proved less than rosy. The board sent Edward Kennedy off to the frontier to face the challenge head on. Kennedy learned the realities of Alaska first-hand so he could serve the unique marketplace.

75

2000
NWC receives Retail Council of Canada
Resources Protection Recognition Award
for Loss Prevention Program.

2000
NWC receives Canadian Diabetes Association
Lawson Award, for achievements and significant
support in the fight against diabetes.

>>

I'D PUT ON MY JEANS AND MY NAME TAG AND JUST BLEND IN.
PEOPLE APPRECIATE THAT YOU'RE TAKING A PERSONAL INTEREST
IN WHAT THEY DO, AND THEY START TO TALK ABOUT THEIR
FAMILY AND THEIR JOB AND WHAT THEY THINK OF THE STORE.
THAT'S WHEN THE REAL LEARNING STARTS.

Board member Jim Oborne puts it in stronger terms. "The reality was that we had put a lot of money into places where we probably shouldn't have. Rightly or not, we regarded Alaska as Edward's problem. So there was a certain amount of pressure on him to make it right. We didn't spell it out for him but I'm sure he understood that he had to fix Alaska or the CEO job wouldn't be his when he got back."

So Edward Kennedy, like many young Nor'westers before him, packed his gear and headed off to the frontier. There was a lot at stake, and he knew the board members would be watching his every move. But he wasn't nervous. He viewed it more as a big adventure. "I hate to say it, but the board guys had more to lose than I did. I didn't feel like my career was on the line. After all, I was only 32 years old. I didn't have a career."

When he and his family stepped outside for the first time in their new home in Anchorage he was "awestruck by the view of Mount McKinley. It was right in our backyard, and all around us were mountains and ocean. We ran out to the deck, as if we might never see this vista again, and promptly locked ourselves out of the house. We had decided to live in a rural neighbourhood, so we had to walk quite a way to find the next house to knock on the door and call a locksmith. Our kids were still very young — Grace, the oldest, was only in Grade One and we were getting them ready for bed — but they were old enough to be embarrassed to

show up at a stranger's door in their pajamas."

One of Kennedy's first priorities was to get out to meet store staff, talk to the customers and get to know the challenges with each location. "There's the tradition of the 'royal visit,'" he says. "The store manager will spruce up the place and the brass will parade in for a quick tour, then they leave and everything goes back to normal. I wanted to avoid that. You get a more accurate impression if you stay for three or four days. By noon of the second day the staff no longer care who you are. They just appreciate the fact you're helping mark the merchandise, put up cans on the shelf, bag groceries or take out the garbage. (I don't work the checkout because that's beyond my skill and I'd be dropping tens and twenties all over the floor.) I'd put on my jeans and my name tag and just blend in. People appreciate that you're taking a personal interest in what they do, and they start to talk about their family and their job and what they think of the store. That's when the real learning starts."

Kennedy toured the stores, getting to know them inside out. ("I was away from home constantly.") The main challenge in Alaska was to beat the competition — to build customer loyalty with the right items, better service and the lowest local price. To the average shopper it might seem like a simple formula, but retailers know that it's one thing to say "more for less" and another thing to pull it off in a complex, high-cost business like northern retailing.

A young family returns from early morning shopping at the AC Value Center in Dillingham, Alaska, October 1997.

**2000**
NWC forms partnerships with RadioShack Canada, H&R Block and TruServ Canada Cooperative Inc.

**2000**
Wintering Partners Conference resumes in Winnipeg.

## WELOME TO PILOT STATION

*Pilot Station is a small village (pop. 650) in rural Alaska, and it's not easy traveling there and back. Villagers use snowmobiles in winter, boats in the summer and ATVs all year long. Fuel costs to run these machines are very high, so the residents of Pilot Station were happy to get their own store in 1973. The store was owned and managed by a native-owned corporation, and although it strove to provide a basic service to local residents, it had little surplus cash for maintenance and improvements. Today, Arthur Heckman is the native leader of the community, and he says the store was run down, had little variety and often sold stale-dated food. He was instrumental in negotiating a new agreement with The North West Company (through its subsidiary, Alaska Commercial) and in January 2011, Pilot Station became part of the AC family of stores.*

*"Arthur worked very hard to make this store happen," says Rex Wilhelm. "The community is a little smaller than what we're accustomed to, so we weren't entirely sure we wanted to get involved. But Arthur is a very determined guy, and thanks to him, Pilot Station now has a great store and it's become a real success story."*

*"The people of Pilot Station love the new store. They just love it," says Arthur Heckman. "We don't have to travel out of the community to shop anymore, so we save the $150 that used to be spent on gas."*

*He says Alaska Commercial can get great prices on food and general merchandise because it buys in large volume and it passes those savings on to the people of Pilot Station. "AC has all the items anyone could want, and they have longer hours, and they are great about keeping things in stock. There's lots of variety, and they sell food products in bulk, which is really important for us. All in all, the new store has made it much easier for low-income families here to access healthy food."*

*The State of Alaska has a government-subsidized food program called the Women and Infant Children Program (WIC). Pilot Station has about 70 WIC clients and Heckman says that having the Alaska Commercial store means that no one has to leave the village to fill their WIC lists. "The AC store is very aggressive in providing families with the WIC needs. They also carry a good supply of hardware and kitchen appliances, and eventually we hope they will be selling clothing and outboard motors and snow machines. We have a plan underway to expand the store in three to five years and add a deli, and everyone is very excited about that."*

## A FEW GOOD MEN

Kennedy says that it was imperative to bring in people with the necessary skills to complement the core team at AC and who really knew American shoppers and American retailing. "I persuaded the board that we needed to hire Jerry Bittner and Dick Hodge. I called them the 'two amigos.' No one can accuse me of ageism because these gentlemen were on the back nine of their careers, but they had incredible energy and they each gave us 10 years of excellent work. Jerry Bittner was like an older-generation version of Ralph Trott — a hard-driving merchant filled with enthusiasm and ideas. He had to learn about the north, and he made a few mistakes because of that. But he had a passion for getting sales, and that's what we needed."

Kennedy addressed Bittner's unfamiliarity with the north by teaming him up with younger executives such as Rex Wilhelm, who had been with Alaska Commercial since 1984, and really understood what was involved in owning and running stores in rural Alaska.

Dick Hodge, the second hire, was an operations man. Kennedy says that when Hodge saw "how dirty the Alaska Commercial stores were, he was afraid that we were going to poison people. I pointed out that we were better than the competition, but Dick said 'That's not good enough.' From a food safety standpoint, Dick made sure we took nothing for granted and that we made a very honest assessment of what we were good at and what we weren't."

Ian Sutherland says many of the directors on the board were impressed by Kennedy's decisions in Alaska. "First of all, he was open to admitting that he was wrong. If selling Alaska Commercial turned out to be the right thing to do, he was open to letting it go. But his primary focus was to turn it around. And he was very smart to bring in Dick Hodge and Jerry Bittner. They developed a very competitive style of operations, designed for that unique Alaska marketplace, and Edward kept building on that. Once he had the core group in place, he began hiring and training more high-quality people and the team began to perpetuate itself."

ABOVE: Edward Kennedy meets with the ACC Executive team. Clockwise from right: Jerry Bittner; Robert Galosich, VP of Wholesale; Edward Kennedy; Dick Hodge and Rex Wilhelm. OPPOSITE: Pilot Station AC Value Center, 2011.

79

**2001**
NWC receives Conference Board of Canada Award for Excellence in Workplace Literacy (National Winner, Large Business Category).

**2001**
NWC receives Manitoba Business Award (Lieutenant Governor of Manitoba Award) for Outstanding Contribution to the Community by a Manitoba Business.

EVERYONE IS A NEIGHBOUR IN A SMALL TOWN. WE LET COMMUNITY TRADITIONS DEFINE THE FEEL OF EACH STORE BUT WE STILL TAUGHT BETTER PRACTICES SO THAT WORK WAS AS PRODUCTIVE AS POSSIBLE.

## THE TRAVELER

The remote fly-in village of Shamattawa is located on the banks of the God's River in northern Manitoba. Len Flett was born there, the son of a fur trader who worked most of his life for the Hudson's Bay Company. "I have a bit of Scottish on the paternal side but I'm mostly Cree. During my childhood in the 1940s my dad worked at Cumberland House, Saskatchewan, so that's where I call home. It's considered the oldest community in Western Canada because it was set up as the first inland post for the Hudson's Bay Company over 250 years ago."

Besides trapping furs, Flett's father worked as a dog team driver for the HBC, delivering mail and trade goods between Gillam, Manitoba, and York Factory. "He was eventually sent to Bearskin Lake where he built a trading post that still stands to this day as an active part of one of our North West Company stores. We spoke Cree at home and my father spoke a number of other Indian languages; he was never able to pick up Dene, which is very difficult. I was young, which helped me learn the language, so I assisted him in the store with our Dene customers."

Flett went to residential school in Powerview, Manitoba, and at one point didn't see his parents for three years. When he got out of school in the early 1960s he worked at a number of odd jobs, mostly construction. One year he went to La Ronge, Saskatchewan, to work on a construction project but arrived too early, so he asked for a short-term job at the local Bay store. The manager told him that in fact Flett's father needed a clerk, would he be interested in that? Flett quickly agreed and without informing his father, boarded a supply plane the next day and flew out to his dad's remote store. "I got off the plane and said, ta-da! How do you like your new clerk?"

Flett says that "temporary" two-week job turned into a 42-year career with the HBC and The North West Company. "I was somewhere in middle management at head office in Winnipeg when the new owners took over. When Edward came in I was promoted to vice president of store development. Edward of course was from the north and hyper-educated, but had less experience with remote Indian communities. I had all the community knowledge but just a high school education, so we formed a team. Our task was to negotiate with First Nation communities and set up lease agreements for new stores on reserve lands. It was a very complicated, very difficult undertaking and required a lot of traveling."

Historically, the HBC had built most of its trading posts and stores next to waterways, off-reserve to obviate the necessity of negotiating land use agreements with the bands. "When the HBC had disagreements with the local Indians they didn't have to listen because they were on their own land, so we inherited a long history of tension and difficult relations. Air travel of course was the new reality, so we wanted to build our new stores on-reserve, next to air strips and roads. So it was our job to negotiate the new leases."

Flett says that when he arrived with his briefcase he might have been regarded as an "apple" (red on the outside and white on the inside) but for his reputation as a supporter of aboriginal interests. "I was quite well known at that time as someone who had always dealt fairly and had opened many doors for First Nations people, in employment and training within the company. So they were ready to accept me as one of their own. I found the process a bit ironic, because they usually had white lawyers representing them and an Indian guy representing the company."

Flett says he had the authority to sign agreements right on the spot. "It impressed the chiefs that I didn't have to call home. In the end, we did something like 40 leases, which meant going to maybe 150 meetings, with the average value of around two million dollars per project. So it was a very exciting job — the best part was being able to put all this development into the hands of First Nations and make it a win-win arrangement for both native people and The North West Company."

During his impressive career, Len Flett helped to generate $100 million in on-reserve assets and 500 new jobs for First Nations members in 100 communities. His efforts in creating partnerships, alliances and joint ventures made NWC the largest private-sector employer of aboriginal people in Canada. He is a recipient of the Order of Manitoba (2012) and the Order of Canada.

WHEN YOU TAKE AN ORGANIZATION APART, IT TAKES
TIME TO PUT IT BACK TOGETHER. YOU HAVE TO LISTEN,
SET EXPECTATIONS AND GET PEOPLE WORKING TOGETHER.
THEN YOU HAVE TO BE PREPARED FOR SOME THINGS
GOING WRONG.

## COMMUNITIES AND PEOPLE FIRST

Kennedy says that getting Alaska to its full potential depended on an entire team approach but that one longstanding strength was AC's approach to community relations. "At that time we did lots of community relations work in both northern Canada and Alaska. The key people were our store managers, our district managers and, at a senior level, Rex Wilhelm in Alaska and Len Flett in Canada. Len was aboriginal, spoke Cree and had years of experience running stores; that gave him a lot of credibility in northern communities. We spent time meeting with local leaders and eventually this led to signed leases and negotiated agreements, most with aboriginal entities. On occasion communities would receive competing proposals from southern retailers. But they rarely invested the time that we did to listen and understand what the community needs truly were. During that era over 40 agreements were reached and without them we wouldn't have moved forward building stores and continuing to grow with the north."

Kennedy says at that time the company began investing in its people by developing training programs that could be self-taught in the northern stores in both Canada and Alaska. "The modules were geared towards store managers and employees. They taught skills but did not impose a 'big company' way of doing things. We didn't expect our cashiers to all start saying, 'Have a nice day,' to every customer because that's not going to happen. What will happen is respectful silence, or a genuine smile, or a shared laugh or a conversation between friends — after all, everyone is a neighbour in a small town. We let the traditions and even mannerisms of the local culture define the feel of each store but we taught better practices so that work was as productive as possible."

Alaska Commercial was soon showing progress. But rumours of The North West Company's troubles still passed between stock traders, business columnists and armchair critics within the company. Bad news is always more interesting than the other kind, and as Mark Twain put it, "A lie can travel halfway around the world while the truth is putting on its shoes." At one point, Bittner and Hodge had the interesting experience of going to Winnipeg for a company meeting, attending a Jets NHL game and listening to the two North West employees seated in the company seats in front of them talk about how "those new guys at Alaska Commercial had better be good because we're tired of propping up their business."

Kennedy heard the gossip, but he wasn't losing sleep. Like a lot of young men, he was indifferent if not dismissive of conventional opinion, and in any case he was convinced the team was doing the right things. "When you take an organization apart, it takes time to put it back together. You have to listen, set expectations and get people working together. Then you have to be prepared for some things going wrong. The skeptics were looking at what the share price was doing over a few weeks or a few months, but our job was to set the stage for improvement and growth that

83

**2001**
The first Giant Tiger store is opened in Thompson, Manitoba, under a test agreement with Giant Tiger Stores Ltd.

**2001**
Alliance with Dufresne Furniture & Appliances begins.

>>

would happen over the next 5 or 10 and 15 years." He adds that there was no specific time when "the clouds parted and the sun came out" and it became clear that Alaska Commercial was going to survive. But after two years, the board decided that Alaska Commercial was now well enough to consider bringing Kennedy back to Canada.

## FINDING A NEW BOSS

At the same time, the board hedged its bet by searching for outside CEO candidates. Oborne, a colourful and outspoken man who functions as the board's chief raconteur, was on the search committee. "At one point we hired a big-time Toronto search agency and they found some people. We went to Toronto and interviewed these three guys, and after the interviews I said, 'I wouldn't hire any of those characters to run a three-house newspaper route.' And the other members agreed with me."

Iain Ronald, the former head of the Hudson's Bay Company Northern Store Division, an old-school HBC man, had long experience with the division, and was perhaps the most seasoned merchant on the NWC board. (He had been invited to join the board because of his executive experience with the northern stores and because he had retired from The Bay around the closing of the transaction.) Oborne says that he and Ronald then went to Anchorage to see Kennedy. "Edward was doing such a good job up there and there'd been enough of a turnaround that he was back in the good graces of the majority of the board. We interviewed Edward and I felt even more certain that he was by far the best candidate for the job." So after more than two years in Alaska, Kennedy came back to Winnipeg to serve as the new CEO of The North West Company. At the board level, Iain Ronald stepped down as chairman, and Ian Sutherland moved up, adding this role to his already long contribution as a director, CEO and the largest individual founding shareholder."

Kennedy had been on trial and passed, but he didn't feel any particular relief at being summoned back from the wilderness. If

anything, he left Alaska with a twinge of regret. "I really enjoyed working with the people at AC," he says. "I learned so much about small stores and northern customers. If I hadn't done that stint, I wouldn't be where I am today. All in all, it was a tremendous experience for my family and me."

Back in Winnipeg, his new task was to build on the work of Trott and Sutherland, starting with the Canadian northern stores. "Overall we were a solid business, we were much stronger than in 1987 and we knew how to defend. But Derek Riley's billion-dollar vision was still in front of us. Our opportunity was to shift our mindset to growing 'with' the North and its young population base while at the same time growing 'within' the North by adding new products and services at a faster pace."

His successful stint in Alaska earned Edward Kennedy the CEO position and a deeper understanding of doing business with people in the north. OPPOSITE: A supply ship arrives in Pangnirtung, Baffin Island, c. 1960s.

**84**

**2002**
Master Franchise agreement signed
between NWC and Giant Tiger Stores Ltd.

# LET'S GO TO SPAIN AND BUY A SHIP

*Don Coles is one of those old-timers who started as a teenager working for the HBC in the Arctic, made the transition to The North West Company when the northern stores were acquired by Ian Sutherland and his fellow investors and now, more than 50 years later, still works part time for the NWC. Coles has had so many adventures during his career that it would take a book to recount them all, and in fact he's writing one. Of his many skills, Coles knows the ins and outs of marine shipping. Most people would be wary about buying a used car. Coles knows how to buy a used ship.*

"Originally the HBC had two or three of their own ships to supply the northern stores. This was costing them a lot of money so it was decided that they would sell their ships and buy the service from other transportation companies. Well, then shipping rates in the north went sky high in a short period of time and insurance was a terrible problem. Up north there are no docks. Everything is barged to shore at high tide, so there were all kinds of damages and our claims got so high that I convinced the board that we should get back into the shipping business and buy our own ship."

His first purchase was a smaller vessel that sailed out of Montreal and came equipped with a captain. "It was about a thousand tonnes and it served us well for a few years. But we needed a bigger ship. By now Ralph Trott was the CEO and Edward doing development work. We got approval to buy one and off we went to Europe. It's not easy buying ships because they are always moving. They don't make any money sitting still, so you no sooner get to a port and you'll find out it's just sailed off to another country. You have to quickly examine it while it's offloading because the captain is not going to sit there wasting time while you check it over. We started in Hamburg, Germany, and then chased off to Spain and then went all over Europe. We must have seen 20 or 30 ships in 10 days."

He was accompanied by North West's sole sea captain and an engineer who knew the back end of a boat from the front. "We kicked the tires on all these ships and our engineer went through the log books. If a log book is falsified at any port, it's a criminal offense. So they go through that, and they check the thickness of the steel and all that. Then you take it on dry dock for further inspections. The final stage is trying to convince Canada Transport to come and see the vessel. They don't like doing that and don't do it very often. Before you can operate it you have to bring it up to Canadian standards. It's worked out very well for us. Under the HBC the marine division lost money, but we now own four ships and we've turned them into profit centres. We send them over to Europe and reflag them in the off season and they earn money for us year-round."

### CHAPTER FOUR

# PUTTING IT ALL TOGETHER

THE COMPANY HAD A LARGE COHORT OF COMPETENT
SENIOR PEOPLE WHO HAD PRODUCED STERLING RESULTS,
BUT THEY WEREN'T GOING TO BE AROUND FOR MUCH LONGER.
NORTH WEST NEEDED NEW STORE MANAGERS AND RENEWED
LEADERSHIP AT ALL LEVELS.

It was spring of 1997 when Edward Kennedy returned from Alaska. He had been in Anchorage for more than two years and, on the surface, everything seemed to be looking pretty good for The North West Company and its new subsidiary. Alaska Commercial had been stripped down to its chassis and rebuilt, piece by piece — new infrastructure, new learning programs, new management, new business plan and a new name for the stores — AC Value Center. AC wasn't yet performing on a par with the Canadian stores, but Kennedy was sufficiently confident to leave it in the care of Rex Wilhelm, Jerry Bittner and Dick Hodge, who still reported to Kennedy, albeit from several time zones and thousands of miles away.

"The North West Company was healthy in terms of profitability," says then-outgoing CEO Ian Sutherland. "We had done a lot of refocusing. We had gotten rid of our junior department stores and modernized our small community stores. Profits were at a peak and I guess you could look at the situation and think that things couldn't be better."

But The North West Company was facing a number of new challenges. The needs of the north and its customers were continuing to change. The company had a large cohort of competent senior people who had produced sterling results, but they weren't going to be around for much longer. North West needed new store managers and renewed leadership at all levels. Given that it was facing limited opportunities for traditional growth in the north, and more competition from a variety of directions, the company decided to meet this challenge head on, by hiring a new generation of aggressive young employees.

Derek Riley says that the drive to recruit new employees wasn't a question of impugning the competence or dedication of the veterans. "A lot of these long-term managers were extraordinary individuals," he says. "Their loyalty was intense, and hard to imagine by today's standards. You can almost picture some of these northern store managers sleeping in HBC monogrammed pajamas or getting 'Hudson's Bay Company' tattooed on their chests. They were extremely dedicated men."

**2002**
NWC launches Best Practice initiative to increase efficiency, produce higher per capita sales, reduce shrink, develop better labour and expense management and lower inventory.

**2002**
NWC receives Winnipeg Chamber of Commerce/Economic Development of Winnipeg Business Award-Education Partnership of Excellence.

## STRENGTHS AND WEAKNESSES

Riley points out that their strength was also their weakness, in the sense that they belonged to an era that was fading. "Nothing much changed in the north for a long period of time, then things started changing very quickly. And of course The North West Company had to evolve just as quickly in order to survive. As the Chairman of the board I kind of set the example by pushing myself out the door. I came in as Chairman in 1987, at the age of 65, and chaired the board for seven years. When I was 71 years old I said to the board, 'I think we should have mandatory retirement at 70 years of age. Because we don't want guys toddling around the board room at the age of 90, saying, what's the name of this company again?'"

The directors agreed with Riley's age cap suggestion, but hoped he wasn't thinking of applying the rule to himself. "They suggested a grandfather clause for my chairmanship, but I told them I didn't think my continuing chairmanship was in the best interest of the shareholders. However, I agreed to stay on for one more year. After I resigned in 1994 they continued to invite me to dinners and meetings and to solicit my opinion on different matters, but I said, 'Listen, you need some young blood. I'm out.'"

Jim Oborne says that in order to bring new people into the company it was necessary to retire some of the veterans. "One of Edward's first priorities when he took over as CEO was to work with the board and his human resources team to design a benefits program that would enable people to retire at 55. It was quite a decent package. We erred on the side of generosity because, listen, they were going to be pensioners and we were very grateful to these individuals. It wasn't their fault that the economy was

Kennedy's dedication to Alaska paid off: the Company earned the intense loyalty of its staff in the north, including Jerry Bittner (opposite), and profits were healthy, says Ian Sutherland (above left).

89

**2002**
Len Flett, VP of Store Development and Public Affairs, receives National Aboriginal Achievement Award.

>>

NOTHING MUCH CHANGED IN THE NORTH FOR A LONG PERIOD OF TIME, THEN THINGS STARTED CHANGING VERY QUICKLY. AND OF COURSE THE NORTH WEST COMPANY HAD TO EVOLVE JUST AS QUICKLY IN ORDER TO SURVIVE.

changing and the company was entering a new phase. It was just a reality, and we had to change with the times. These gentlemen had done an excellent job and we had a friendly or at least collegial relationship with them. Some of them didn't want to retire, so we had to let them go and that was difficult. And I think it was hardest on Edward, because he wanted to get costs down and modernize management but now he had to do the dirty work, similar to Alaska.

The retirement and recruitment program was the first task in what would prove to be a long and complicated reconstruction job. Eighty-five people left from the Winnipeg head office and 50 from the northern stores. Ian Sutherland says the company needed to prove that it could grow. "We knew it would be disruptive to retire a large number of people but the future of the company was at stake. Yes, we were profitable. But the earnings weren't growing. Our sales were $447 million in 1992, and had only grown to $474 million in 1996. That's a steady increase, but percentage-wise, it was below market."

Kennedy says that the reduction of personnel "bought the company some time and money to introduce a new direction." Traditionally, the typical northern store had the ambiance and appearance of a small-town general store. Tools, frying pans, fishing tackle, duct tape, nails and assorted general merchandise dominated the hardware section of the store. In the clothing

Northern store staff and managers take pride in consistently offering fresh food to their customers. LEFT: A customer checks out at the Northern store in St. Theresa Point, 1996.

91

2002
NWC receives March of Dimes Award from Society for Manitobans with Disabilities, for its commitment to hiring and training people with disabilities.

2002
NWC receives Cornerstone Award from United Way Winnipeg, acknowledging contribution of more than $100,000 to its campaign.

>>

THE STORES STILL LOOKED AND FELT LIKE THEY DID 20 YEARS BEFORE, CARRYING A LITTLE BIT OF EVERYTHING. IF WE WERE GOING TO MEET THE EVERYDAY NEEDS OF OUR NORTHERN CUSTOMERS WE WERE GOING TO HAVE TO GET SERIOUS ABOUT PUTTING FOOD FRONT AND CENTRE.

department, racks were stocked with long underwear, denim jeans, work boots, rubber boots, joggers, spring jackets, winter jackets, headwear, mitts and gloves. Some of the racks were dedicated to fashion clothing. But, as Kennedy points out, it's hard to compete with larger southern stores on selection. "You can never provide enough variety for a community of a thousand people. If you are going to have a proper apparel selection with sizes, colours and styles for both men and women you're talking about hundreds of unique items. We obviously compete with the Sears catalogue, or with shopping mall stores or the internet, so we decided to downsize areas like this and go in a new direction — food."

Traditionally, the northern stores placed a secondary emphasis on food. But in terms of the customers' everyday needs and the store's revenue per square foot, food was much more important than general merchandise. Also, the demand for food was growing. "Our markets were full of young, large households with equally large food-spending needs," says Kennedy. "The stores still looked and felt like they did 20 years before, carrying a little bit of everything. If we were going to meet the everyday needs of our northern customers we were going to have to get serious about putting food front and centre."

## REPROFILING

Paul Smith worked as a manager in several stores (mostly the Rossville store, in Norway House, Manitoba) until he was asked to come down to Winnipeg in the early 1990s to work in HR as a "content expert" on the company's store training modules. He became one of the new generation of store people who moved to Winnipeg to help with upgrading the northern stores. "Because I was young, I thought I was a natural expert in everything you needed to know about running a store. But it was a great learning opportunity to find out that maybe I didn't know it all from having worked in my remote spot in Rossville. After a few years in the training department, I moved on to operations as the accountant and technology specialist for the Interior Region — which at that time was the James Bay area, Northern Ontario and Manitoba. Basically, I was going out to the stores to help them with their systems."

Smith became the director of store systems, which meant he was responsible for computers and point-of-sale systems, and he spent considerable time in Alaska, working with Rex Wilhelm to put in place upgraded software and hardware. "We went around to all the stores, making sure we were helping them out or at least

A Northern store in Arviat after reprofiling, 2001.

92

**2003**
Iain Ronald, former Chairman, retires from Board of Directors after 16 years of service.

**2003**
NWC receives March of Dimes Award from the Society for Manitobans with Disabilities, for its commitment to hiring and training people with disabilities, for the second year in a row.

# THE MAN BEHIND THE COUNTER

*Paul Smith started with the Hudson's Bay Company in 1979, as a bag-boy in Pinawa, Manitoba, then went to La Loche, Saskatchewan, as a management trainee. "My boss told me, 'you know, we're going to invest a lot of money in you, you better stick it out.' And I stuck it out just fine for the next 25 years. I managed a number of stores, and my favorite posting was my 5.5 years in Norway House where I ran the Rossville store. You'll hear lots of stories about the HBC neglecting the northern stores, and I think they were just very out of touch with our division. You'd see them getting off the plane in their suit jackets and neckties, all hunched over and shivering in the snow, and everyone would chuckle because they looked so unhappy to be stuck up north doing another store tour. Meanwhile the store managers were being quite entrepreneurial, without much support from these folks from The Bay."*

*Like northern store manager Don Coles, who experimentally ordered a massive planeload of fruit without permission from his district manager, Paul Smith took the approach that when it came to local initiatives, it was easier to apologize than to seek permission. "We often did things without asking. When I was in Rossville, we had an empty metal warehouse that I turned into a convenience store. I made a couple of counters out of plywood and some Plexiglas we had lying around. We stayed open late, and sold gasoline, candy, pop and other convenience store kind of items. I remember a senior manager from Winnipeg showing up and telling me it took nerve to do something like that without asking permission. But we were making money so he didn't have much else to say about it."*

*Smith gradually worked his way up through The North West Company and ended as a Vice President in charge of Information Services. But he remembers his managerial days in the northern stores with fondness, and still has unequivocal respect for store managers. "When I started out in 1979 we had to stamp cans with prices, and trust me, when prices changed, they had to change more than a couple of cents for me to go back out there, scrape those labels off and re-price the tins of Alphaghetti! Then we had to learn the whole automation system with bar codes, and explain those bar codes to our staff and customers. Then in the 2000s we evolved to wireless in-store systems hooked up to a satellite, and going from those extremes in a mere 15 years was akin to evolving up from the dinosaur age. But the store managers, like all northerners, are great adapters, and they made the transition without a hitch. They were the real heart and soul of the company, and they still are."*

not hurting them. Our efforts eventually paid off and we got the systems running smoothly. And I guess Edward was pleased with the results because he asked me to lead the reprofiling project, which was a real challenge."

Smith says the new assignment meant he was "soaking up an awful lot of knowledge in a short period of time, and the project affected the whole organization, because reprofiling was about making choices on what to sell and not to sell in our stores so that we could grow faster. The decision was to put more selling space into food because our data showed we were fighting a losing battle to out-shopping in general merchandise and were missing opportunities in food. So we were repositioning the stores to be more food-centric, because it's tougher to order in a pound of hamburger than it is a pair of fashion jeans and you buy hamburger a lot more often."

Smith's team also worked on "planograms," which meant that the design, inventory and shelf layout of each of the northern stores would still be designed around customer needs but would for the first time be organized on the shelf using centralized expertise. This approach had several advantages. "Not least of them was creating a consistent image and a defined set of looks in each store. It meant we would be able to tell our suppliers exactly where their product was going to be placed on the shelf. It meant putting brand new freezers and coolers in the stores, and being able to say 'This four-foot section of the cooler will be dedicated to selling these items with the right space and position to each one.'"

Smith says that for the senior people at North West, reprofiling the stores also meant reprofiling their own attitudes about northern retailing. "When the company decided that food was now the first priority, it brought abrupt changes to the layout of the store. But it took more time for that changeover to seep into the awareness of our store managers and our senior managers at Gibraltar House. So we worked hard, actually out of a basement room at Gibraltar House, to address everyone's questions and it took about 18 months before everyone from senior management

**2003**
NWC receives Canadian Diabetes Association's Outstanding Corporate Partner Award, for an innovative alliance to bridge a corporate partner and the CDA.

down to the store managers was comfortable, that, yes, this was what we wanted to do. After that, it probably took another two or three years before we were all really committed to improving how we planned, bought and sold food. Reprofiling was a major change of direction for the company and affected a million square feet of selling space. A major move both in terms of where merchandise was presented in the stores, and a major move in the way we defined ourselves."

When customers walked into a reprofiled Northern store in the early 2000s they saw aisles of new food items — specialty and "value" branded cereals, rice and canned goods and more than double the previous space allocated to perishable items, from yogurt to frozen entrees to fresh produce and meat. There

were now fewer but still a range of key basic clothing and general merchandise items. Instead of being a general store that also carried food, Kennedy explains that the Northern store was now a food store that also carried a wide range of general merchandise. "When we changed the focus to food, we took apparel off the floor and put it up on what we call waterfall racks, where it cascades down and you see the front of the first tee shirt or blouse and the rest are behind that. It's very space efficient, and space in a Northern store is prime real estate."

Inevitably, store reprofiling generated both positive and negative reactions in the community. And some of the disappointment was non-specific and visceral. Having grown up in the north, Edward Kennedy understands the respect that

With more competition from southern business, NWC's operations gained an edge by listening to the needs of its communities. The inventory of today, including a wide range of food and clothing options, starkly contrasts with the basic offerings in decades past.

95

**2003**
Ivan Ahenakew Award presented to Edward Kennedy
by the Interprovincial Association on Native Employment.

>>

northerners maintain for the traditional way of doing things. "There's a comfort and affection that many of our customers and staff have for the way we have always done business. You can still find almost anything in our stores. We still carry that roll of duct tape and that outdoor extension cord and that box of coated nails. We're proud of being counted on as an everyday needs store and customers will still say, 'If the (Northern or AC) store doesn't have it, you don't need it.'"

**2003**
Sandford Riley joins Board of Directors.

**2004**
NWC receives National Recognition Award from Certified Management Accountants Canada-Manitoba Partner, for meeting and exceeding the philosophies associated with service to the profession and to the economic development of Canada.

REPROFILING WAS A MAJOR CHANGE OF DIRECTION FOR THE COMPANY AND AFFECTED A MILLION SQUARE FEET OF SELLING SPACE. A MAJOR MOVE BOTH IN TERMS OF WHERE MERCHANDISE WAS PRESENTED IN THE STORES, AND A MAJOR MOVE IN THE WAY WE DEFINED OURSELVES.

## PROFIT IN PERISHABLES

In terms of community demand, switching space and skill to food made sense. There were also other benefits, like the faster turnover of food compared with general merchandise. Less obvious was the company's ability to deliver fresh food consistently. The average observer might suppose that general merchandise is easier to transport than food — especially in the north, where winter temperatures can stall at minus 40 for weeks on end and transportation glitches are the norm. And it's true that the challenges of transporting fresh produce — let's say a banana, from its producer in the tropics, way up in the backcountry of the Rio Magdalena, Colombia, for example, to its consumer who may be strolling down the aisle of a Northern store in Pond Inlet, Nunavut — are mind-boggling. But here again there was a tradition and expertise that could be built on. Don Coles worked as a manager in a variety of northern stores for many years, and he says that keeping remote communities supplied with fresh fruit and vegetables is not as horrendous a task as one might think. "It's a long way to some of these communities in terms of miles, but you have to remember that many of them have air strips, and there might be aircraft coming in every day or every couple of days."

Coles says that he and other Northern store managers experimented with bringing in fresh product. "This was back in the 1960s," he says, "and in those days the HBC store managers were completely on their own. They decided what they were going to sell, when they were going to sell it and so on. Sales were increasing rapidly during that period. Hunting was extremely good and the Inuit art business was excellent, so there was a lot of revenue around. So I ordered a DC-3 loaded with 7,000 pounds of fresh produce and the plane arrived on the same day my divisional manager arrived from headquarters in Winnipeg. He came only twice a year, so this DC-3 rolled up and I thought maybe I was going to get fired. He was so upset because no one had ever done this before. But thank goodness, I had kept the Inuit posted on what I was ordering and they had saved all this money in their accounts, and three hours after the plane left, I don't think there were a dozen eggs left in the store."

Coles says that was an important lesson for his professional development as a retailer and later, as a transportation specialist for The North West Company. "That's when I realized there was a great demand for all kinds of foods that the Inuit people had never seen before. Northerners are very adaptable and open-minded. In that harsh environment it's a survival necessity to keep your eyes open and keep learning about new things every day, and I learned that there is no bias against new fruits and new food products. And it's very rewarding to offer something and see it snapped up by eager customers. It makes your day, just to see their happy faces."

**2004**
NWC opens first retail pharmacy in Iqaluit, Nunavut.

**2004**
Northern Pharmacy (Ontario) Inc. launches Canada's first Telepharmacy program to provide professional hospital pharmacist services in Weeneebayko Hospital.

>>

... IT'S VERY REWARDING TO OFFER SOMETHING AND SEE IT SNAPPED UP BY EAGER CUSTOMERS. IT MAKES YOUR DAY, JUST TO SEE THEIR HAPPY FACES.

Edward Kennedy adds that perishability is a challenge for all retailers, no matter what they are selling. "Clothing styles change every season, and hard goods like computers and iPads and even snow machines go out of date quickly. That's where the risk lies. In the city, you can mark an item down every week until you find the right price that sells. In a small northern community there are only 500 to 5,000 people in the market and when you have too much of an item, or the wrong item, there's a good chance you won't find anyone locally to buy it, at any reasonable price."

The transition from general merchandise to food was costly and difficult and didn't happen overnight. The company first lowered its costs by reducing its payroll and becoming leaner and more efficient. Those initiatives freed up dollars to invest in the food business. As Kennedy explains, "we phased in the change, by putting an emphasis on hiring people who had come from a food background. Fresh produce will only sell well if you have the right equipment, so we invested in that area."

Aboriginal owned and operated airlines such as Air Inuit are part of the finely tuned systems that bring fresh food into the north, including an impressive meat selection.

**2004**
Next-generation store systems are installed in 137 stores, completing the Northern Canada and Alaska rollout that began in 2003.

**2004**
NWC starts direct importing from China, launches motor vehicle sales and opens new gas-bar formats.

>>

WHEN YOU CONSIDER THAT MANY OF OUR STORES ARE IN REMOTE LOCATIONS, AND THAT THEY VARY CONSIDERABLY IN THEIR SIZE AND THE TYPES OF MERCHANDISE THEY HANDLE AND THAT WE HAVE TO SHIP BY WINTER ROAD, BY SEALIFT, BY AIR AND SO ON, IT WAS SOON CLEAR THAT NO ONE REALLY PROVIDES A SIMILAR SERVICE TO OURS.

## FINDING A DISTRIBUTION CENTRE

Don Coles says that the move to food required new systems of warehousing. "As we grew into food, our warehousing needs increased rapidly. Our first food distribution centre was a 50,000-square-foot building on Church Street, and that was totally inadequate for our needs as a nation-wide food retailer. One of my major tasks in our new North West Company was to build a new automatic distribution network, which required a cost-effective and time-efficient order processing method while servicing our stores."

So, like a sea creature that quickly outgrows its shell, the company was rapidly evolving. When Ralph Trott took over in the late 1980s, most of the senior managers freely admitted that they didn't know how to turn on a computer, let alone handle computerized spread sheets and complex tracking and ordering programs. "Our warehouses in Montreal and Toronto were very inefficient," says Don Coles, the boy-clerk from Newfoundland who spent half his life in the Arctic and eventually became the company's go-to expert on storage and transportation. "They were labour intensive, paper-based and had a very slow throughput rate. They were simply unable to handle the growth that North West was planning to take on."

Under orders to fix the logjam and fix it fast, Don Coles set out across North America on a hunt for the very best state-of-the-art computerized warehousing system that money could buy. "We needed to close two centres," he says, "one in Montreal and one in Toronto, and replace them with a single, highly efficient centre that would operate at much lower cost, so this was no easy assignment. I secured the services of a materials handling consultant from Cleveland and visited eight major distribution centres across the United States. When you consider that many of our stores are in remote locations, and that they vary considerably in their size and the types of merchandise they handle and that we have to ship by winter road, by sealift, by air and so on, it was soon clear that no one really provides a similar service to ours. Nevertheless, we did our homework and came up with a technology solution."

The $12.2 million Winnipeg Logistics Service Centre opened in April 1993. With its combined softgoods and hardgoods distribution capability, and its automated merchandise handling equipment, the warehouse easily sorted small packages and earmarked them for the company's diverse and far-flung stores. Just as remarkable is the makeup of the centre's staff. When the North West warehouse closed in Montreal, the veteran workers there faced a tough choice — stay in cosmopolitan, vibrant Montreal (and look for new jobs) or keep their jobs with North West and move to the prairie city that some Montrealers and Torontonians like to call "Winterpeg." A remarkable number chose

**2004**
Three new Giant Tiger stores opened, bringing number of stores to 10.

**2005**
Order of Canada presented to Len Flett, VP of Store Development and Public Affairs.

With an international network of stores and extensive inventory, the Company invested in distribution technology. OPPOSITE: Product arrives by ship to AC Value Center stores. ABOVE, FROM LEFT: Donna Rattray (right), Production Manager, Distribution, explains the high-tech equipment to an impressed group during one of the tours on opening day, April 2, 1993; A computerized carousel bringing the items to the worker was an example of the new automated merchandising equipment at the newly opened Retail Service Centre in April 1993. The centre was later renamed the Winnipeg Logistics Service Centre.

to move to Winnipeg, and although that was a striking display of loyalty to the company, it was also a testament that in some ways Winnipeg is Canada's best kept secret.

Colin Wiltshire was one of those warehouse employees who made the move. He says he's definitely a loyal Nor'wester, but the move to Winnipeg wasn't entirely devoid of self interest. "Sure, Montreal has good restaurants and culture and so on, but that's all a bit over-hyped. The fact is, so does Winnipeg. As a place to live, Montreal was flatlining and there wasn't much future there, given the political problems and the relatively stagnant economy. And as far as I'm concerned, you can't be poking fun at Winnipeg winters if you live in Montreal. In contrast, this city is booming. There's zero unemployment and nice, affordable housing, great cottage country nearby, friendly people, tons of culture and lots to do. My basic reason for moving here was because North West is an awesome company. But Winnipeg was a great bonus, and I'd do it again without hesitation."

**2005**
NWC opens pharmacy in Inuvik, Northwest Territories.

**2005**
*CashLink* debit cards introduced, eliminating costs when handling cash, vouchers and paycheques.

>>

## SERVING THE NEW CUSTOMER

David Chatyrbok thinks it's important to point out that, although North West is now a food retailer first, it has also refined and improved its approach to selling general merchandise. Chatyrbok joined The North West Company in 2000, and is now the Vice President of Procurement and Marketing for Canada. His responsibilities include food, but he has also put a lot of time into upgrading the company's approach to selling general merchandise. He says it's not just a matter of keeping stores stocked with bingo dabbers, socks and batteries. "Over the last 10 years, the internet has spread all across the north, and social media have become an important information source. Our customer is always up to date with southern trends. Whether it's fashion or iPods and tablets, northern consumers are right up to speed. For example, Facebook has one of the highest penetration rates in the country, and that's connected northerners to the buzz around new products of all kinds."

Says Chatyrbok, "We really pride ourselves on being up to date — whether you're talking about new and different cereal flavours or electronics or even transportation. Our customers are fast movers. There is no isolation factor when it comes to information. And that makes our job more exciting and more challenging."

It's one thing to declare an intention to "beat the competition" but how does North West win against big-box and online retailers who don't pay the heavy costs of operating or investing in the north and, consequently, can provide the same products at lower prices? "We have to stay ahead of them on the right products, on service and on keeping the total price, including freight, in range," Chatyrbok says. "And believe it or not, we do exactly that. We do it by talking to our customers and tracking their needs. We never stop looking for the next great item, and making sure that we have it in the right quantities."

The company's search for the "next great item" is expensive and time consuming but it's necessary. Chatyrbok sends teams of "cool hunters" off to China on a regular basis to see what's coming up in innovative digital products. "We never did that

## STORE TRAINING

*In many communities The North West Company's outlet is one of a limited number of local stores. While some outsiders might see that as an opportunity to exploit vulnerable customers, many First Nation leaders give North West credit for its attempts to improve the quality of community life. Don Robertson is a religious leader and Metis elder who grew up in Norway House, Manitoba. He says North West has been an important partner in that community's development. "I always told them the most important thing was to hire local young people and train them, not just as clerks but as store managers and as people who can work elsewhere too. And the company has done a good job of that. There are far more native people working in the northern stores than there used to be."*

*Cathy Salter started her career working as an assistant manager (in Moosonee, Ontario) and worked her way up to a position as Senior Manager of Organizational Development at the company's Winnipeg office. She is a northerner by birth (raised in Sudbury) and is a strong advocate of the company's commitment to partner up with the people it serves. "North West is continually striving to find and train employees from the local communities. Managers understand that it's in their store's interest to hire locally. Locals know the language, they know what's going on in town and they have credibility with the customers. The stronger the employee base you have in your store, the stronger the store is as a true service to the community. It typically starts with a manager noticing some responsible young person in the store and approaching them with a job offer. If that employee is motivated and serious, there's no limit to how far they can go."*

*Salter says that store managers take great satisfaction in training young people. "When I managed the store in Cross Lake, I hired a young First Nations lady named Nadine Garrick as a part-time cashier. And it was patently obvious after about three days that she had way more potential than just being a cashier, so we moved her into managing a department on the general merchandise side, looking after menswear. That wasn't enough to keep her busy, so we gave her a grocery section as well; she was only about 20 years old. So I called my boss in Winnipeg and said, 'we have to hang on to her because she shows tremendous promise.' We did an interview and offered her a position in our store-manager training program. In time, she took over our store in Waskaganish and became one of our first female, aboriginal store managers. Then she and her husband wanted to move to a more urban setting, so now she's an assistant HR manager here in our Winnipeg office."*

*A visit to any North West store will uncover such stories. Todd Nadeau, the Director of Recruitment and HR Services for North West, says the company has made good progress in its campaign to become "the people's store" in the north. We've always been strong in hiring and training local people for entry positions. In Canada alone, about 2,800 of our northern store employees (more than 80 percent) are First Nations people, Inuit and other northerners. Where we've made a bigger improvement is increasing the number of northerners working in management positions. This started in the 1990s and is now at 20 percent of our total management ranks."*

when I joined the company 12 years ago. But now we send our buyers over there regularly to seek out the best products and get the best pricing that they can. The cheaper we can source products the greater savings we can pass on to our consumer."

North West buyers get to know their customers in many ways, from asking for new product comments on Facebook to spending time in the north. As Chatyrbok explains, "these are carefully selected communities that represent large customer regions. The buyers might pick a First Nations community for their spring and summer trip and an Inuit community for their fall visit. When they're in the community, they're working in the store and visiting customers to ask questions and study their everyday activities and lifestyles."

One of the most important sources of advice for all head office staff is ongoing feedback from the stores. Weekly reports are sent in by store managers and provide an invaluable snapshot of trends, issues and selling opportunities. "This year we are using our website and sites like Facebook to allow our customers to communicate directly with us. We want to get as close as possible to their views whether it pertains to back-to-school items, hunting supplies or food choices."

## THE TOMORROW STORE, AND MUCH MORE

Since joining North West in 1993, Mike Beaulieu says the rate of change within the company has been rapid and unrelenting. "It's really been an exciting ride," he says. "When I came on board, store books and customer-stock ledgers were still done with paper and pen, and we were just making the transfer to a computerized system. I started as a management associate at our new Nelson House store, which was one of our new concept designs, called the 'tomorrow store.'"

Ralph Trott and Edward Kennedy were leading a team of senior people that was revamping the whole company, and Beaulieu says the tomorrow store was designed to be a state-of-the-art northern retail outlet — the right size for the growing community, with high-efficiency shelving and the right product mix for the new directions that the company was heading into. "I then moved to other store assignments and then to Winnipeg as a field manager. Now I'm working with our long-range planning initiatives, which means always staying a jump ahead, for example still having the

**2005**
New fuel-dispensing
stations are added.

**MARCH 2005**
Jerry Bittner, President of
Alaska Commercial, retires.

WE HAD GROWN A GREAT DEAL ACROSS THE CANADIAN NORTH AND INTO ALASKA, TO THE POINT WHERE THERE REALLY WASN'T MUCH ROOM LEFT TO GROW GEOGRAPHICALLY. BUT THERE WAS STILL ROOM FOR DEEPER EXPANSION WITHIN THE COMMUNITIES WE SERVED, AND OFFERING FINANCIAL SERVICES WAS PART OF THAT.

right goods on the shelf for when a customer's out looking for them but doing it in a way that is more productive after factoring the high cost of utilities, equipment and product waste. Growth is an ongoing dynamic and it never slows up. During my time we've grown from phone to fax to internet to the type of fast-paced electronic intelligence that we have today. For me, this constant effort to improve and sustain the business is the most exciting part about being with North West."

Adding new stores in new markets was of course a major way to grow the company's footprint. But North West continued to investigate ways to grow internally, as well, by multiplying the goods and services that each store could offer. Brian Fox was a key player in these "intrapreneurial" initiatives, which in his case involved the expansion of financial services. "We had grown a great deal across the Canadian north and into Alaska, to the point where there really wasn't much room left to grow geographically. But there was still room for deeper expansion within the communities we served, and offering financial services was part of that."

Fox says this move into financial services wasn't a case of North West trying to sell a service that wasn't needed. "People in the north have trouble getting access to conventional banking services. Our idea was to offer people the range of practical, dependable banking services they were asking for — cheque cashing, ATM service, money transfers, cash cards and even income tax preparation."

As Fox points out, the northern store had always been a sort of informal banker in northern communities, going back to the days when fur post managers would give trappers equipment and food staples as an advance on future fur sales. "Trust and credit have been part of the way we do business in the north. So we started to automate the processes behind the relationships by putting in ATMs and offering cash cards and prepaid cards, and our own debit cards, all of it run on technology that connects with the store using high-speed internet, over a phone line or, in the far north, it may be a dish on a 20-foot tower pointed at a satellite far to the south.

"Then we created a product called 'Link.' Customers can load their paycheques or their social assistance cheques onto their electronic cards, then withdraw cash or use the Link service to transfer money to relatives in the south. And of course no one wants to keep large amounts of cash lying around in the house so a Link account is a safe place to keep money."

Computers, as everyone knows, can be temperamental, but Fox says they've made the system foolproof. "You can't have your store shut down so we have built more redundancy than we need. In every project I've been involved in we always planned for catastrophic events."

Link Financial Services include gift cards, tax services, and debit and credit cards.

**109**

MARCH 23, 2005
Rex Wilhelm appointed President of Alaska Commercial.

2005
Sales start for motor vehicles, complementing the lineup of snow machines, all-terrain vehicles, boats and motors.

>>

# ROAD STORIES

*With all due respect to the "100-mile diet" movement, many of the items in the typical North West Company food store come from far away. This is by necessity — the cold climate and barren soils of the north make it difficult or impossible for northerners to produce their own milk, cheeses, beef, eggs, fruit, vegetables and other ingredients for a healthy, varied diet. So these foods must be freighted in. If you walk though the produce section of a NorthMart store, you might feel that it's the same as any southern, urban food store. But it's different in one respect — all those red apples, plump oranges and crisp heads of lettuce have come a long way. And if they could talk, here are some of the stories they might tell:*

*Let's look at the example of a shipment of bananas bound for Baker Lake, Nunavut. After being harvested in their country of origin (usually in Central America), bananas are piled into boxes, stacked onto skids and loaded onto ships and trucks bound for North America. Several days later they arrive at e NWC's Crescent Multi-foods perishable depot in Winnipeg where they are ripened to the appropriate stage. The bananas are then loaded onto another truck and shipped north to Thompson, Manitoba, where they are transferred once again to a train and hauled north to Churchill. There, they are packed onto a plane to Baker Lake and then loaded onto a truck at the airport for the shortest, but still costly, leg to their final destination.*

*In order to preserve their freshness during the northward journey, bananas are wrapped in an insulating produce blanket and put in a special temperature bin. But anything can happen along the more than half dozen different modes and "touch points." On one occasion, an airport freight handler who was loading the bananas on a plane thought they would get too hot, so he left the lid off the bin, and the bananas produced condensation, which froze. When the fruit got to Baker Lake, it was rock hard and stuck to the floor. Having learned his lesson, the baggage handler sealed the box on the next load, turned off the freezer vent and the bananas arrived in liquid form. And North West picks up the costs of mishaps along the route.*

*Fresh meat must be shipped quickly from the processing plant to the store. Temperature control is critical because hamburger only lasts eight days. And during winter road season the truck journey itself may take more than four days, depending on the weather and the ice conditions. One year the ice road to St. Teresa Point was in such bad shape that the truck could only get part way, at which point the local people unloaded it by hand and hauled the store goods to the community by snowmobile and toboggan. Another year, a truck carrying five tons of freight to Norway House hit a snow bank and tipped over. The community turned out and unloaded the truck by hand. The only thing that broke was a jar of spaghetti sauce — because someone dropped it.*

*The winter roads are temporary routes built largely on frozen lakes. Lakes are better than land because lake roads are flat, but truckers must drive carefully. A heavy truck depresses the ice (which is often two meters thick) and pushes a wave ahead of it beneath the ice. If the truck moves too fast it will overtake the wave and crash through the ice. The most dangerous part of any winter road is near the shore, where a wave entering the shallows can break the ice from beneath, causing a "blowout." Good ice "talks back" with a chorus of loud gunshot cracks and groans as the truck crosses it. Bad ice is silent. In dangerous conditions, a trucker will often drive with the door open.*

*With all the risks and costs and effort involved in delivering food to remote communities in the north, it's no wonder that tropical produce like firm, fresh bananas cost more in the store than they do at the source.*

LIKE WINTER ROADS, AIR CARGO INTO THE NORTH ADDS TREMENDOUS COMPLEXITY AND COST TO SOMETHING URBAN CANADIANS TAKE FOR GRANTED EVERY DAY: HAVING FOOD ON THEIR STORES' SHELVES.

With 'intrapreneurial' efforts, The North West Company stores have become a one-stop shop for everything from fuel to pharmaceutical services. ABOVE: Refuelling at the Quikstop in Iqaluit, 2008. OPPOSITE: Shannon Beck, Pharmacist at the Northern store in Moosonee, Ontario, 2009. PREVIOUS: A First Air 767 in Iqaluit, Nunavut, offloads merchandise bound for the Iqaluit NorthMart.

Of its many skills, North West is especially adept at dealing with misadventure. As Rex Wilhelm puts it, "when you're doing business in the north you get accustomed to the likelihood that something is going to go wrong."

That "something" might be a massive wind storm in northern Saskatchewan that takes out the phone lines. On the same day, a forest fire could burn through the wires in another community. Winter is a blizzard season in the north and typhoon and hurricane season in the company's southern Cost-U-Less markets and store hours are often affected by both. Brian Fox says the company limits the damage by assuming that trouble is never far away. Like the aviation business, North West builds redundancy into the way it works. "For example, without our backup credit card systems, a store's internet could be completely isolated for a week

or more, but people still need to be able to buy their groceries. We've set it up so you wouldn't even know whether the store was offline or not. It's called a 'store and forward' system. The store continues to record all of the transactions and once the link is re-established, all of the transactional history comes through and we're able to complete credit billings and all the rest. We have that backup for every store."

Another "intrapreneurial" initiative has been to add fuel outlets says Edward Kennedy. "We were at first hesitant because fuel dispensing is expensive and requires stringent procedures to protect against spills and contamination. We eventually figured out how to manage the risk and now selling fuel is a good investment. When people stop to buy gas, they go inside and buy a few more items. It all comes down to making the store an everyday, helpful

**2006**
Acquisition of retail pharmacy in Moosonee, Ontario.

**2006**
Partnership with Bailey's Furniture begins..

PATIENTS WILL BE ABLE TO GET THEIR MEDICATIONS THE SAME DAY THEY ARE NEEDED, WHICH OF COURSE IS VERY IMPORTANT. THE BIG PICTURE IS THAT PEOPLE WILL HAVE ACCESS TO QUALITY HEALTH SERVICES IN THEIR OWN COMMUNITIES.

part of community life. If there's a need that's not being met, we'll see if we can partner with the community to provide it."

One of North West's recent initiatives has been a pharmacy program. Dalbir Bains joined the company in 2008 as the Vice President of Planning and Corporate Development. (Essentially the same role Edward Kennedy took on when he was hired by Ralph Trott.) Bains explains that the pharmacy and other medical services initiatives grew out of the company's determination to expand the services it provided within each store. "I was assigned to assist the company in driving new growth initiatives. The company had already decided to introduce pharmacy services in our northern locations, and when I came aboard, North West owned seven outlets. Northerners in the past often had to get by without this basic health service. Even communities of four or five thousand people sometimes have no pharmacist, so this seemed like an unmet need and a good opportunity for us. But these pharmacies lacked consistent standards and our first priority was to make them solid, service-driven operations and then expand into other communities."

Bains worked with his team to make the pharmacy program more effective and grow the service. "North West now has 12 pharmacies and has improved the bottom line significantly. They offer different levels, ranging from full-serve in-store pharmacist in large stores to having prescriptions filled from a central hub location and sent out to customers living in communities of 2,000 or less."

Northern hospitals access after-hours and emergency pharmaceuticals dispensing through North West's "Telepharmacy" program, in which the nurse or technician contacts an NWC on-call pharmacist based in the south and requests review and approval of a prescription. Bains says the company is working on innovative systems in which automated devices, coupled with a video phone for consultation, will dispense drugs in the same way that an ATM dispenses money. "That will really blanket the north with pharmacy services," he says. "Patients will be able to get their medications the same day they are needed, which of course is very important. The big picture is that people will have access to quality health services in their own communities. This will not only save enormous expenses in flying people back and forth to medical centres, it will save people who are already experiencing medical difficulties the stress, inconvenience and loneliness of having to leave their families to access basic care."

He says that First Nations are becoming involved in the pharmacy program as full partners of North West. "First Nations and Inuit people are the bulk of the clientele in the north, so it makes sense for them to partner in these initiatives. One of the biggest challenges facing northern communities is economic development, and the pharmacy program is a way for First Nations to reduce their costs for pharmaceuticals and repatriate revenue and jobs for their communities."

116

2006
New North West Company brand rolled out with men-in-canoes logo replacing the old beaver and tree motifs.

2006
Edward Kennedy receives Retail Council of Canada's Distinguished Canadian Retailer of the Year award.

# FINDING THE LIFE I WAS LOOKING FOR

Angele Raymond grew up in a small town in Northern Ontario, and as a teenager, worked for the local pharmacist as a clerk, helping to fill prescriptions and working at the front of the shop. "I really enjoyed being with the customers," she says, "and before long I decided that I wanted to become a pharmacist. Once I graduated from high school, I moved to Montreal where I completed my Bachelor of Pharmacy at the University of Montreal."

After five years in Montreal, Raymond missed the friendly atmosphere of small town life, and moved backed home to begin her career as a pharmacist. After several years of work, adventure beckoned, and she moved to Senegal, Africa, where she did volunteer work for two years. "It was exciting and challenging to learn a different culture and a different language. When the time came to return to Canada, I wasn't keen on the idea of returning to my same old job. I wanted to do something more challenging, and if possible, to work in an inter-cultural setting."

She saw a posting for a pharmacist job at the North West Company store in Iqaluit, and thought, "That sounds perfect! From sunny Senegal to chilly Nunavut! I must be nuts!!!"

Reminding herself that she was "the tough little girl from Northern Ontario," Raymond applied for the job and was accepted. "Isolation and snow don't really scare me. So in April 2005, I climbed aboard an airplane in 35 degree-plus weather and began a journey that ended in 35 degrees below zero in Iqaluit. When I got there it was snowing. I had tears in my eyes because I hadn't seen winter in two full years! That just wasn't right for a Canadian! I was a little nervous because I hadn't worked in a standard pharmacy setting for so long, but I was also excited to see my workplace and meet my colleagues, and very much looking forward to learning about the community."

Raymond says it didn't take long to learn that life in the Canadian north is not so different from life in the developing world. "It was really similar in some ways to Africa. All of a sudden, shipping became a huge part of my daily worries. Will we be getting our order today? Will the medication for that patient arrive on time? Will the planes be flying out? Or will we be facing a blizzard or a mechanical problem? Are we packaging the medication properly to prevent it from freezing? So, yes, being a pharmacist in the north presents all sorts of logistical problems. You are constantly thinking ahead and devising innovative ways to address problems that a southern pharmacy would never have to face. It adds spice to your everyday routine."

Not long after she moved to Iqaluit, Raymond bought a snowmobile and a 4-wheeler. "Believe it or not, I've never really been an outdoor type of person, but when in Iqaluit, do as the Iqalummiut do. Now I'm out there on the ski-doo in minus 40 degree weather, and really enjoying it."

She took up fishing in the summer, and says she enjoys that too. "There is nothing more rewarding than catching your own dinner. The beauty of living here is that you can go to work for the day, but still have time to enjoy all of Iqaluit's activities because it doesn't take you an hour to commute to and from work. And instead of sitting in a car, stuck in traffic, you can actually drive your 4-wheeler to work. Now that's the life!"

Raymond also joined the Community Choir, the Badminton Club and the Racquet Club. "Yes, I have time to do all those things, because life here is at a much slower pace than in southern cities. It doesn't take you all weekend to run your errands. So you actually have time to live and enjoy your friends and take part in all sorts of activities."

When Angele Raymond moved to Iqaluit, she says she planned to stay for two years. "But I'm still here after six and a half years and I'm not planning on going anywhere. I really enjoy it here. My work is still challenging, even after all this time, and I have lots of time to do the things that I like. I guess you could say that I found the life I was looking for."

IT ALL COMES DOWN TO MAKING THE STORE AN EVERYDAY, HELPFUL PART OF COMMUNITY LIFE. IF THERE'S A NEED THAT'S NOT BEING MET, WE'LL SEE IF WE CAN PARTNER WITH THE COMMUNITY TO PROVIDE IT.

## PARTNERING WITH FIRST NATIONS

Grand Chief David Harper grew up in Garden Hill, a Cree Community in northern Manitoba, where his grandfather and his father trapped furs and acquired goods at the local HBC trading post. "My grandpa and my dad were very good fishermen, hunters and trappers. They caught lots of beaver, lynx and marten and made good money, so we never lacked for anything and there was lots of food on the table. My three older sisters went to residential school and when they came back they went to work for The Bay northern store. The northern store was part of the fabric of our community, and it was pretty much the only place in Garden Hill you could get a full-time position."

Harper says his father taught him and his brother many outdoor skills, but he didn't want both his sons to work in the bush. "He raised my brother to be a trapper and woodsman like himself, and mainly pushed me towards getting a good education in the south and getting a profession. I don't know why he made those choices but that's what he wanted. So I went into aviation management and got my commercial pilot's license and flew planes for a while. I didn't want to fly in the bush. I wanted to be a corporate pilot, so that's the direction I went in, and by the time I was 30 years old I had a good job working as the General Manager of Perimeter Aviation.

"That experience with Elijah Harper and the Meech Lake Accord taught me a valuable lesson," says Harper. "It wasn't threats or blockades that stopped Meech Lake. It was one man working from inside the system. It showed me that you can get way more done working from inside than from outside. So when I was in my early 30s, and was asked to run for the chief of Garden Hill First Nation, I was determined to apply that lesson and cooperate with outside businesses to the extent that it served our needs and advanced the cause of economic development. During my 10 years as Chief of Garden Hill, I did a lot of business with The North West Company. There are no banks in rural communities, and North West was the only company that could handle our financial needs — money transfers, cheque cashing and so forth. So we used The North West Company a lot. And combining that with the business experience and public relations skills I'd learned at Perimeter Airlines I was able to get a lot of things done during my 10 years as Chief."

In 2009, CEO Edward Kennedy addressed the chiefs and leaders of Manitoba Keewatinowi Okimakanak (MKO) at one their regular meetings. His intention was to introduce MKO to North West's ideas on health joint ventures and to measure their interest in partnering up with First Nations to bring related jobs and economic development to their communities. Harper says the chiefs had difficulty getting past old issues. "They were stepping into him over the price of food and general merchandise and many other grievances about the Hudson's Bay Company. Even though North West has been a separate company for 25 years there are still a fair number of people in the north who think the NWC is The Bay. And there's a lot of history between The Bay and native people, some of it good and some of it bad. Some people are still telling stories about the time a trader took advantage of their grandfather, and Edward Kennedy was getting the brunt of that."

2007
Edward Kennedy receives University of Alberta School of Retailing's Henry Singer Award for Exceptional Leadership in the Retail Sector.

2007
The North West Company receives Outstanding National Corporate Award from the Canadian Diabetes Association.

Food is an important and pressing issue in the North. In 2011, Executive Vice-President of Northern Canadian Retail Michael McMullen spoke to the Nunavut Legislature about the Nutrition North Canada Program.

In 2010, Harper invited Kennedy to meet his chiefs again, this time at the MKO executive meeting in Pukatawagan. This time, he says, the chiefs were more open to Kennedy's message. "We made it clear that we want to be business partners in every aspect of northern development. We did that with all the regional airlines. Perimeter, Calm Air and now Bearskin all signed agreements with us and we became part owners. And now we are very interested in getting involved in the delivery of health care."

## CONNECTING WITH COMMUNITIES

As a retailer that specializes in serving remote, often economically disadvantaged regions North West deals with social responsibility in a serious way. Says Edward Kennedy "from the board level right down to the store manager we understand our duty to deal fairly with the customers we serve and, wherever possible, to create employment and bring revenue into the community."

When it comes to the food that The North West Company stocks on its shelves the company strikes a delicate balance between two, sometimes conflicting, goals: providing healthy foods and giving customers what they want. Jim Oborne is characteristically frank about this difficult issue. "We're genuinely trying to sell healthy food. Having said that, you can't fight your customers. Some people are always going to want chips and poutine and all that crap. But we're going to be there with healthy eating choices."

Isn't it true that selling junk food is more profitable than selling healthy products? Says Oborne, "There's no question that there's more profit in selling a litre of soda pop than a litre of milk. And some people might argue, 'Look, you guys are running a business. It's not your job to tell people what they should be drinking and eating. It's your job to be the best at giving customers what they really want and to make money for your shareholders.' Well, that might be the opinion of some people but it's not the view of The North West Company. We had one director who made that argument and we asked him to leave. And that argument

DECEMBER 2007
NWC acquires Cost-U-Less.

2008
Sandford Riley appointed Chairman
of the Board of Directors.

WE'RE BUSINESSPEOPLE, BUT WE SERVE SMALL COMMUNITIES AND
WE ARE VERY SENSITIVE TO THEIR NEEDS AND THEIR PRIORITIES.
WE AND THEY HAVE AN INTEREST IN PROMOTING HEALTHIER FOOD
OPTIONS AND TOGETHER WE WORK ON MAKING THIS HAPPEN.
IT'S NON-NEGOTIABLE THAT WE MAINTAIN AN ETHICAL,
SUPPORTIVE ROLE.

has never been made before or since. We're businesspeople, by and large, but we serve small communities and we are very sensitive to their needs and their priorities. We and they have an interest in promoting healthier food options and together we work on making this happen. It's non-negotiable that we maintain an ethical, supportive role."

David Lui is the Director of Marketing Services for North West. One of his job responsibilities is to increase sales for the company, but he feels no conflict between that mandate and the drive to help people to make healthy choices in their shopping habits. "We're not just a company," he says. "We're also active members of the communities where we operate. Our customers are our neighbours and our friends. That's not the case with most city retailers. Our store managers know the families, know the kids, and they have a stake in keeping that relationship positive. The healthier the relationship, the healthier we all are."

Edward Kennedy says that when it comes to living choices, NWC is always looking at trends and new products. "One of our programs teaches how to shop for a healthy meal at an affordable price. We provide menu and meal preparation information, both on our website and in-store. We encourage people to consider shopping for canned items that can combine with fresh product to make a very healthy, nutritious meal at a much lower cost than

going right to the frozen food aisle for your entire meal."

In its ongoing effort to foster healthy living, North West maintains active working relationships with a variety of governmental organizations like the Canadian First Nations Inuit Health Branch, different departments of northern development and aboriginal affairs, and diverse provincial state and territorial health agencies. Local tribal governments, the Canadian and American Diabetes Associations, and the Heart & Stroke Foundation also work with The North West Company on community health issues. "One simple way is through our role as community gathering place," says Edward Kennedy. "The northern store has been a meeting place since the beginning of the fur trade. A big challenge for health and other government agencies is getting their message out since it's too expensive to travel everywhere in person to deliver their programs. Our stores are a great conduit for passing on information. We sit down with the agencies and talk about educating customers and they're surprised at how much work we've done already. We can help them through brochures, posters, school visits, sponsoring events and through our weekly advertising."

David Lui adds that North West contributes a share of its profits to healthy living programs in the community. "We sponsor hockey teams, dog sled races, marathon runs and other athletic

2008
Core Principles developed: Thinking Customer
Driven, Passion, Enterprise, Accountability,
Trust and Personal Balance.

## WORKING FOR THE PEOPLE OF THE NORTH

*The Hudson's Bay Company always had good luck recruiting young men from the islands of northern Scotland. They were familiar with isolation and rough weather, had a good work ethic and, luckily for the Company, didn't have a lot of career options.*

*In the summer of 1965, the HBC hired Jim Deyell and 41 other young men from the Shetland Islands. "I'd heard about the Canadian north at an early age," he says. "So when the HBC did a recruiting sweep I was very pleased to be selected as a trainee clerk. They loaded us onto a DC-8 and flew us to Montréal, Winnipeg and Edmonton, where they x-rayed us, checked our teeth and general health, issued us northern clothing and told us where we'd be going."*

*Four days after leaving Scotland, the 17-year-old Deyell arrived at Coral Harbor, on Southampton Island. He found that the small arctic community had a similar culture to his own village. "With the ocean and the subsistence fishing and hunting, it felt like home. If someone had extra fish or if they'd caught a seal they'd share it, just as we did. I studied the Inuit language and learned it well enough to carry on a conversation. The northern life captivated me and, except for a failed attempt to join the RCMP, I worked in the northern store network for the rest of my career."*

*Deyell went on to work in Cambridge Bay, the Belcher Islands and other posts. He learned to pull teeth, give needles and deliver babies. "That sort of work endeared me to the people," he says. "We were cut off from the outside world for long periods, and you just had to do your best. I became very close to the Inuit folks, and still am — with the people of the Belcher Islands in particular. Shortly before I retired, I told Edward, 'You know I'm not really working for The North West Company. I'm working for the people of the north.' I think he appreciated that."*

# RUNNING FOR
# HER PEOPLE

*"I didn't tell people I was doing this because my father always told me to be humble, and not draw attention to myself."*

*Her secret ambition was to be a marathon runner, and several years ago, inspired by the example of Terry Fox, Rick Hansen and other champions for health awareness, she got the idea of combining her love of running with her concerns about diabetes. "Diabetes awareness is a major campaign of mine," she says. "It's become almost an epidemic in First Nations communities. We used to work hard in the bush and live off the land, eating good wild meat and wild foods. Now too many First Nations people are inactive and eat a lot of processed foods with sugar in them. I have an auntie and uncle who are both diabetic, and four or five of their kids, also have the disease. In 2010 I told my family and friends that I was going to enter a marathon in Orlando, Florida, and that I was going to be running and raising money for Team North West, which participates in marathons around the world to raise awareness of diabetes."*

*Bibianna King went to Florida and ran two back-to-back marathons — the half-marathon on the Saturday and the full marathon on Sunday — and raised $4,000 for diabetes research. "So that was an experience and a challenge," she says. "But the scary thing for me was going to Rome. I looked at the map and thought, oh my god, am I actually going there?"*

*She had to raise a minimum of $3,000 to cover her expenses, and managed to surpass that with $3,700 in sponsorships. (North West matches pledges on a dollar-for-dollar basis, and any surplus goes to diabetes education and research.) "Some supporters gave me five hundred dollars and some gave me much less. But each gift firmed up my willpower. You can't imagine how inspiring it is when a child walks into your office and gives you her own dollar, and tells you she believes in you. I'm so grateful to all of them, and in my mind they were sitting alongside me as I flew to Rome."*

*King now organizes marathons, walks and diabetes awareness projects in her home community. "I ran with Edward Kennedy and David Lui and other members of The North West Company in Rome and they are great supporters of what I'm trying to do at home in Portage la Loche. Our marathon is called The Long Sun Run, and last year was our third year. We had over two hundred people participating, and The North West Company paid for the medals, they paid for our banners, they paid for our food at the finish line and they paid for all of our water and Gatorade. They've been really great supporters of this community and our campaign to beat diabetes."*

endeavours. Last year we spent $1.3 million on these types of activities and we try to practice what we preach. We built an excellent gym in our Winnipeg head office and it's getting busier and busier with people working out and staying fit. The cafeteria offers healthy food choices at subsidized prices and it's a big hit with visitors to the building. I've been with North West for three and a half years and I've found this emphasis on healthy living to be very inspiring. I've lost 35 pounds since I came here and spiritually and physically I've never felt better in my life."

## ON THE RUN FOR HEALTH

In 2001, a long-time North West Company employee named Jim Deyell started a remarkable campaign to get the company directly involved in the campaign against diabetes. Deyell, who came over from Scotland as a boy to work as a clerk in the northern store network, traveled extensively in the north during his career with the company and ended up being a District Manager. He lived and worked in remote communities where hunter-gatherers were making the difficult switch from natural high-protein, low-sugar diets to a "modern" diet of processed fatty foods, soda drinks and candies, and he saw first-hand the terrible impact it was having on their health. Deeply troubled by this, he installed a coin collection box for diabetes across the stores in the James Bay District. That initial mini-project raised a surprising $3,500, and inspired Deyell to continue with his fundraising efforts. "I guess the most important thing I did was challenge our CEO Edward Kennedy to set an example for everyone by going and running in the Rome Marathon," says Deyell. "He trained for it, joined Team Diabetes (a diabetes awareness charity group) and completed the marathon that same year and raised almost $100,000. That inspired other employees, and it has grown into a very successful team effort for The North West Company."

Not all the participants are employees. "You can apply to join Team 'North West' Diabetes at any of our northern stores," says Lui. "You fill out an application form and if you are chosen, we'll match the sponsorship funds you raise."

In 2011, on the 10th anniversary of Edward Kennedy's solo effort, a team of 77 North West Company employees, associates and

**2008**
NWC wins Asper School of Business
Co-op Employer of the Year Award.

community members returned to the Rome Marathon. (Among them were Grand Chief David Harper, Edward Kennedy, David Lui and other senior Nor'Westers.) The Rome Marathon is one of the largest in the world, and that year it drew more than 16,000 entrants. Thousands of spectators cheered wildly as the participants ran, walked and wheeled past the ancient Coliseum and other historic sites. Many of the NWC team members knew diabetics and had even lost parents, brothers or close friends with diabetes, and their dedication was visible and passionate. That year they raised approximately $500,000 for the Canadian and American Diabetes Associations, adding to the million dollars-

plus that everyday NWC employees and northerners have raised for diabetes education, treatment and research since Jim Deyell decided to install a coin donation box in the Moosonee store.

"We're just retailers," says Edward Kennedy. "But we can inform and even inspire others. We can't drag customers by the arm down the aisle to the healthy food section and say, 'Here, eat this! It's good for you!' We can't order them to drop to the floor and do 50 push-ups or go for a long jog every morning. But by demonstrating our genuine concern for their health and well being, we can offer a hand and be there, ready with ideas, activities and choices."

125

North West Team Diabetes at the Rome Marathon, 2011.

**2009**
NWC listed as one of 50 fastest growing companies in *Manitoba Business* Magazine.

**2009**
Edward Kennedy receives Top Retail Executive Award from *Canadian Business* Magazine.

>>

### CHAPTER FIVE

# TAKING COMMUNITY RETAILING TO THE CITY

MATCHED WITH GROWTH, ENTERPRISING IS ABOUT ALWAYS LOOKING FOR NEW IDEAS AND CHALLENGING YOURSELF TO DO BETTER. IF THIS ISN'T HAPPENING YOUR BEST PEOPLE ARE GOING TO JUMP.

Eight years after the Alaska purchase and ongoing innovations to the company's Canadian business, its stores were beginning to thrive amidst robust northern population and economic expansion by adding new products and services. With these paths firmly in place the possibility of adding a "third leg" to the enterprise began to take hold. As Kennedy puts it, "by 2000 we had the financial capacity and the bench strength to consider new markets that built on our skills. And in the year 2000 that was the urban south."

Admittedly, this was the same market that the company had gotten out of 10 years before, when it sold off its mid-sized department stores. So Kennedy felt that he had "some explaining to do" to his shareholders. "Since our core business had always been serving remote communities there were questions about what value we could bring to urban markets. It was new, and it was definitely out of our comfort zone. But we kept an open mind and we noticed that one specific type of smaller-sized store — also known as a "junior" discount format — was underdeveloped in western Canada.

In revamping its northern stores, and shifting the emphasis from general merchandise to food, the company had begun to see the possibilities of this expertise being leveraged into other types of stores. "We recruited and blended into our team several merchants and store operations personnel with urban food skills as well as people who were used to handling food in a warehouse environment. It was providing us with excellent returns measured by our rate of same-store sales compared to other food retailers in North America."

The return journey to southern retail began with an opportunity to acquire SAAN stores, another Winnipeg-based retail chain that, by the late '90s, was under severe financial pressure as it attempted to go head to head with big-box stores like Wal-Mart and Superstore. More appealing to North West was a group of viable SAAN stores in medium-sized "mid-north" towns along the fringe of the territory already served by the northern stores. "We put in an offer to buy two-thirds of their stores that had a profitable track record and a solid niche in rural Canada. Our idea was to introduce food and run the stores under our northern banner. In this way, by latitudinal degree we could move through rural markets towards the south. But our offer was rejected. Another buyer came along and within two years they were in bankruptcy."

The failure of the SAAN proposal didn't dampen Kennedy's belief that there were still opportunities to extend North West's reach into the mid-north and urbanized south. But how?

## HOW THE GT STORY BEGAN

Don Beaumont had a distinguished career as the president of K-Mart Canada, after which he joined the board of The North West Company. When North West's offer to purchase SAAN fell through in 2000, Beaumont suggested that Kennedy look at Giant Tiger, a company that Beaumont considered to be one of Canada's greatest but least known retail success stories. As Kennedy recalls, "It was a wise suggestion, and I was intrigued to learn that Giant Tiger's product range was a unique mix of fashion, food and seasonal hardlines all sold in stores only one-fifth the size of a Wal-Mart.

**2009**
NWC launches long-range planning initiative called "More Growth in Store," which positions operational excellence as top priority for the company's retail network.

**2009**
More than 90 percent of households in NWC's remote markets shop in the company's northern Canadian stores every month.

I WAS INTRIGUED TO LEARN THAT GIANT TIGER'S PRODUCT RANGE WAS A UNIQUE MIX OF FASHION, FOOD AND SEASONAL HARDLINES ALL SOLD IN STORES ONLY ONE-FIFTH THE SIZE OF A WAL-MART.

They gave their managers autonomy to order their own products. This allowed Giant Tiger to tailor stores to the local community and get on trends faster than larger, centrally controlled stores. Added together this was a unique and compelling concept and it was worth testing in western Canada."

Jim Oborne was on the Executive Committee that assessed the merits of partnering up with Giant Tiger, and he says they recommended the plan to the full Board for a number of reasons. "Giant Tiger served lower-income customers, and that was similar to our core business. We reasoned that by buying into an already successful business we could manage the start-up risk of going it alone with a brand new venture against large, established players. We also believed that we could further develop our food skills while learning about urban retailing, especially in non-food categories. And it was clear that their buying power, when added to ours, would benefit all of us."

On the negative side was the necessity of sharing effective control of the venture with another entity and the risk of whether there was enough money to be made for both parties. While exploring ways of expanding the northern store market during the 1990s, North West had set up retailer-to-retailer agreements with companies like Pizza Hut, A&W, KFC, Dufresne Furniture and H&R Block. Kennedy says, "By the time we linked up with GT we were a very 'open-architected' retailer, probably more so than any other chain in Canada. GT on the other hand, like our previous retail partners, was used to having control. We reached an agreement that recognized the strengths of both companies, namely our regional food capability and their store model with its emphasis on trend merchandise at great prices."

## TEAMING UP WITH THE TIGER

In 2001 North West launched a test store in Thompson, Manitoba. Says Kennedy, "Because of freight costs, staffing issues, high rent and other challenges we felt that if a Giant Tiger store worked in Thompson it would be a success in many markets in western Canada."

Christine Reimer was hired to manage the second store, in Winnipeg. She comes from a fashion retailing background in Toronto, and says she had no knowledge of or interest in Giant Tiger when a recruiter called her. "I had never even heard of The North West Company, let alone Giant Tiger. And I told the recruiter it didn't sound like my kind of business. But they asked me to keep an open mind and go visit a Giant Tiger store, so I went to see the one in Ottawa, which I think is the first Giant Tiger location. It was quite old and run down. My background was the Gap and Old Navy, which was a different clientele and different business altogether. So I told them, no way, this is not for me."

The recruiter nevertheless felt that Reimer was a good candidate for Giant Tiger, so she met with Edward Kennedy in Winnipeg, who explained the team spirit and enterprising ethos

**2009**
NWC integrates its international network of information systems and buying groups, and opens new distribution centres in new locations in Edmonton, Alberta, and Tacoma, Washington.

**MAY 23, 2009**
First Island Fresh IGA in Guam opens.

of The North West Company. "I was very inspired by Edward," she says. "So I took another look at it, and decided to join the company as a store manager for Giant Tiger. As you know, the Thompson store was the first location. It opened in June 2001, and I opened the second one, on Logan Avenue in Winnipeg, in October of the following year. Winnipeg is my home town, but I spent a lot of time in Toronto, and to be honest, I didn't really know that part of Winnipeg very well. It was a really old location, and I was leery because I was used to working in busy shopping mall situations where people come to you, and I thought, well, I know the Thompson store is doing well, but who's going to come here?"

Reimer got a big surprise on opening day. "I've never seen anything like it. We had lineups outside. We had people pushing through the doors. We actually had to bring in security people to control the crowds and allow people into the store 10 customers at time. It was absolutely crazy. It was October, which is a perfect time to open because we were going straight into Christmas. So I just thought, is this ever going to end? Will we ever have an opportunity to catch up? Before a store opens, during the set-up process, you have lots of time to get organized. But our business was so crazy right off the bat that we weren't really sure how to handle the next steps. The customers obviously loved the store but it wasn't that easy to find good employees to handle the demand. But we did, and I can say that we have at least 10 people in the store that have been there since the beginning."

After the successful openings in Thompson and Winnipeg, North West signed a Master Franchise agreement with Giant

Solo store in Pinawa, Manitoba, 2012.

131

>>

**2010**
Implementation of "More Growth in Store" leads to industry-leading growth in food sales under NWC's northern banners.

**2012**
NWC devotes approximately 1.5 percent of net earnings to community support centred around sports and recreation, culture and arts, healthy living, education and environment.

THEY GAVE THEIR MANAGERS AUTONOMY TO ORDER THEIR OWN PRODUCTS. THIS ALLOWED GIANT TIGER TO TAILOR STORES TO THE LOCAL COMMUNITY AND GET ON TRENDS FASTER THAN LARGER, CENTRALLY CONTROLLED STORES.

I'VE NEVER SEEN ANYTHING LIKE IT. WE HAD LINEUPS OUTSIDE. WE HAD PEOPLE PUSHING THROUGH THE DOORS. WE ACTUALLY HAD TO BRING IN SECURITY PEOPLE TO CONTROL THE CROWDS AND ALLOW PEOPLE INTO THE STORE 10 CUSTOMERS AT TIME. IT WAS ABSOLUTELY CRAZY. IT WAS OCTOBER, WHICH IS A PER-FECT TIME TO OPEN BECAUSE WE WERE GOING STRAIGHT INTO CHRISTMAS. SO I JUST THOUGHT, IS THIS EVER GOING TO END?

Tiger, and began opening stores across the four provinces of western Canada. Says Kennedy, "We signed a 30-year agreement that gave us the exclusive rights to open and operate Giant Tiger stores in Manitoba, Saskatchewan, Alberta and British Columbia in exchange for a royalty payment. And we agreed to work together where we felt we could both benefit. They supply the basic store model, which is everything from the look of the store to the shopping bags to the computer system. We handle the food side of the store. All the non-food items — the fashion clothing and the hard goods — are bought through Giant Tiger and shipped to our stores in western Canada. We have a distribution centre in Winnipeg and recently added one in Edmonton, so we have the capacity to add stores. Overall, it worked really well at the start and has been a harder, but still attractive business to stay in over the past few years."

Jeff Grose is one of the company's veteran employees. He started working in the HBC northern stores in the early 1980s and lived through all the events and shifts in direction leading up to the much-improved retailing enterprise that The North West Company has become today. He says that the Giant Tiger project was a striking example of how North West had matured as a company and gained the strength and agility to "think outside the box." He

was involved in supplying food to the Giant Tiger outlets and says the entire arrangement was initially difficult and challenging. "It was a real puzzle but also very exciting and interesting. When you've been with the company for as long as I have you see many different things, for sure, but one of the highlights was the business with Giant Tiger. It forced all of us to come up with some original ideas and that's what Edward excels at. One of Edward's strengths, for sure, is to consider all the angles and think out into the future, and he foresaw how this volume buying would give us leverage with suppliers. And that helped our northern stores as well, by lowering our costs of acquiring large volumes of food, which of course benefits our northern customers."

Giant Tiger stores in regional centres like Thompson and The Pas, Manitoba, serve the same customer as the northern stores, and in that sense, the venture has been performed, like the potential fit of rural SAAN stores, as a natural extension of North West's traditional market. Shoppers from remote communities will drive or fly to the larger communities in the mid-north to stock up on food and make special purchases of other items where they may once again find themselves shopping at a North West Company store, albeit one that operates under the Giant Tiger banner. In larger cities

OPPOSITE: Customers line up for grand opening deals at Giant Tiger Store 402 in Winnipeg, Manitoba, October 20, 2001. PREVIOUS: Giant Tiger's convenient locations provide shoppers with a unique blend of everyday low prices on basic family and household needs combined with the newest fashions arriving daily.

135

**JANUARY 1, 2011**
NWC completes conversion from trust fund back to share corporation.

**2011**
Tim Hortons debuts in three locations in Iqaluit, Nunavut.

>>

TOP: Edward Kennedy speaks at the grand opening of Giant Tiger Store 423 in Lloydminster, Saskatchewan. BOTTOM: According to one Giant Tiger store owner, "We're the only 'boutique' around that can say it sells both fashions and litres of 2 percent milk!" OPPOSITE: The Cost-U-Less in Curacao, Netherland Antilles, adopted the Casa Manita Orphanage, which is home to 34 boys and girls aged 4 to 15. The store donated books to start a library, organized cleanup events and helped raise funds for a fresh coat of paint.

like Winnipeg and Edmonton, the company's Giant Tiger outlets are often — though not always — located in neighbourhoods where, as Kennedy puts it, "we may be serving relatives of our northern customers."

Other stores serve immigrant communities and new Canadians. "It depends on the neighbourhood," says Oborne. "While our downtown store on Ellice Avenue in Winnipeg has a high component of First Nations shoppers, our first store in Winnipeg at Logan and McPhillips has a largely Filipino customer base, and was hugely successful from day one. It was right beside a SAAN store of similar size, and it did more volume in one month than SAAN did all year. SAAN was gone within a year, and we're still there, and it's still a very busy store."

As a junior discount store, GT uniquely appeals to fashion shoppers (many of them women) who love the fact that they buy trendy new fashion items, right in their neighbourhood, at rock bottom prices. Business professionals, students and homemakers crowd the aisles, sifting through the designer apparel and marching to the checkout with smiles on their faces. A common remark is, "Giant Tiger is my favourite store," echoing the declaration of Gordon Reid, founder of Giant Tiger Stores Limited, that quality merchandise posted at low prices will generate not only sales but gleeful loyalty among shoppers.

At the end of 2012, North West operated 31 Giant Tiger stores across western Canada. And nothing demonstrated the company's growth better than a map of Canada and Alaska, with North West flags waving from the 49th parallel to the high arctic, and from the rocky shores of Labrador and Newfoundland to Alaska's old Russian colonies in the Bering Sea. Nowhere in Canada or Alaska was there a market left undeveloped. It was time for the company to start looking at the rest of the world.

**2011**
Second direct-to-customer food distribution outlet is added to Edmonton distribution centre.

**2011**
NWC's eastern Arctic shipping venture has record-setting year for volumes and revenues.

## TAKING CUSTOMER
## SERVICE TO A NEW LEVEL

*When a tragic mid-winter fire destroyed an apartment complex in downtown Winnipeg, dozens of low-income tenants found themselves suddenly without housing, adequate clothing and even basic essentials like food and toiletries. North West has applied its typical community spirit to the daily operations of Giant Tiger, and the discount retailer moved quickly to donate food, clothing and other essentials. Unlike most of North West's retail outlets, most Giant Tiger stores are located in urban environments, and this foothold gives North West an opportunity to get involved in inner-city community programming.*

*NijiMahkwa school is located in a poor neighbourhood in Winnipeg's north end. It is an elementary school designed for aboriginal kids, and North West employees work there as volunteers. Sarah Gay is one of them. "I started off teaching literacy to the children but ended with 25 new little friends," she says. "We're also involved in other communities, working with Boys and Girls Clubs across the country and we adopted a boarding school on the Caribbean island of Curaçao where we are supporting 70 kids with food, clothing and mentorship. We try to take customer service to the community level."*

*Like many North West employees, Gay is young, energetic and idealistic. Her eyes glow with excitement when she talks about volunteer work. "We're involved in environmental efforts, raising $250,000 for our 'Greener Tomorrow.' We also pitch in with local sports and recreation programs, providing equipment, scoreboard clocks and jerseys. And we recently piloted the North West Run for Diabetes helping to combat diabetes in our communities. I have one of the best jobs in the world as the Community Support Manager. I come to work every day with one question on my mind:  How can we better help our communities?"*

137

### CHAPTER SIX

# FROM PINES TO PALMS

OUR FIELD IS QUITE A SPECIALIZED ONE, AND IT PIQUED MY CURIOSITY THAT THERE WERE STORES LIKE OURS, IN AMERICAN COMMUNITIES LIKE THE ONES WE SERVED, BUT IN THE SOUTHERN HEMISPHERE.

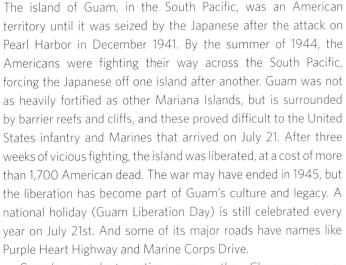

The island of Guam, in the South Pacific, was an American territory until it was seized by the Japanese after the attack on Pearl Harbor in December 1941. By the summer of 1944, the Americans were fighting their way across the South Pacific, forcing the Japanese off one island after another. Guam was not as heavily fortified as other Mariana Islands, but is surrounded by barrier reefs and cliffs, and these proved difficult to the United States infantry and Marines that arrived on July 21. After three weeks of vicious fighting, the island was liberated, at a cost of more than 1,700 American dead. The war may have ended in 1945, but the liberation has become part of Guam's culture and legacy. A national holiday (Guam Liberation Day) is still celebrated every year on July 21st. And some of its major roads have names like Purple Heart Highway and Marine Corps Drive.

Guam's prevalent native group, the Chamorro, were traditionally hunter-gatherers, skilled seafarers who organized their society along matriarchal lines. Chamorro culture celebrates the power and prestige of women, and cultural knowledge and traditions are passed on by legends, music, dance, chants, courtship rituals, handicrafts and preparation of herbal medicines.

In these and other ways the native people of Guam have much in common with many North American aboriginal groups. Guam also struggled over the years to get access to the same goods and services available to other American territories, and large food retailers in particular were slow to open stores on the island.

That situation began to turn around in 1989, when an American entrepreneur named Michael Rose started a store in Hawaii called "Cost-U-Less" (CUL), targeting Americans who came to the islands on extended condo vacations and wanted to fill their larders with Costco-style merchandise. It was a no-frills warehouse, club-style store that offered U.S. branded goods at low prices. To stock his store, Rose bought merchandise directly from Costco in Seattle, shipped it by sea and simply resold it in Hawaii. Three years after the Hawaii store proved itself he took the concept to Guam, where he opened a store in Dededo, the island's largest population centre. His target customers were middle-income locals, businesses and bargain-hunting Americans.

The Guam store likewise proved successful, so he opened another store there, and launched a Cost-U-Less store in American Samoa. One of his employees, Bill Fisher, worked as a

2011
NWC establishes an agreement with Manitoba Keewatinowi Okimakanak, a regional northern Manitoba tribal council, to provide future health services.

2011
NWC's pharmacy division grows to include hospital contract services.

CUL manager for several years before heading north — far north — to take a job with a company called Alaska Commercial. There, he met a young executive named Edward Kennedy. The North West Company had recently purchased Alaska Commercial, and Kennedy had moved north from Winnipeg to get the struggling company trimmed up and running right. Kennedy was fascinated to hear Fisher talk about his work at Cost-U-Less, which to him sounded like an Alaska Commercial store operation, only with palms instead of pine trees. "He actually had a background in remote retailing that didn't include working for us," says Kennedy. "Our field is quite a specialized one, and it piqued my curiosity that there were stores like ours, in American communities like the ones we served, but in the southern hemisphere."

These conversations, and exposure to other former CUL employees now working for AC, inspired Kennedy to start thinking about the South Pacific. "I began studying Cost-U-Less," he says. "I wasn't thinking about buying them necessarily. Cost-U-Less had more geographical breadth than we wanted. I was thinking that we might want to launch a store or a chain of stores in the South Pacific ourselves. So I was studying them, more to learn more about their successes and their mistakes than plan a takeover."

After its initial success Cost-U-Less expanded through the South Pacific and into the Caribbean until it finally opened two stores in New Zealand. That, says Kennedy, "was a bridge too far. Their formula was to purchase American branded product and transport it via American shipping lanes. All their operations were

Cost-U-Less on the Grand Cayman Island, 2012.

**141**

2011
After assessing the way the company moves and tracks products, NWC selects new Transportation Management System (TMS) and lays the foundation for its integration and rollout in 2013.

MAY 2, 2011
NWC begins trading on
TSX under original NWC symbol.

>>

in American territories or countries that had established freight routes to the U.S., where customers were very familiar with American consumer brands and packaged food products. When they got to New Zealand, they overlooked that the country had an established domestic consumer packaged goods industry. Filling a store with American goods that were transported halfway across the world at tremendous expense was a bust with local shoppers. The stores in New Zealand did poorly and had to be closed, and by the late 1990s CUL was under financial stress."

Added pressure then came from Costco, which moved to Hawaii and began competing with Cost-U-Less on its home turf. From his distant perspective in Alaska, and then Winnipeg, Kennedy observed CUL as it struggled through the 1990s, and into the 2000s. He was back in Winnipeg and running The North West Company by that time. Alaska Commercial had grown from 15 to 34 stores. The Nor'Westers had set up a franchise agreement with Giant Tiger and that network of stores was expanding across urban markets in western Canada. So the north was covered and the urban south in western Canada was being developed. Kennedy concluded that a fourth leg of new growth now made sense and that the most attractive place to look was in foreign markets.

## THE OTHER SIDE OF THE WORLD

As the years passed, Edward Kennedy kept his eye on the South Pacific. "I checked on Cost-U-Less regularly to see what was new with them and how they were making out. Michael Rose, the founder, had been diluted down to a small share of the company and was eventually replaced as CEO. Under the new management team, the company was modestly profitable but wasn't showing a lot of improvement. Meanwhile at the back of our minds were the lessons from previous ventures in Russia and Greenland during the mid-1990s."

Perhaps North West's most cinematic failure was its attempt to set up shop in what Ronald Reagan dubbed "The Evil Empire"

THE NORTH WAS COVERED AND THE URBAN SOUTH IN WESTERN CANADA WAS BEING DEVELOPED. KENNEDY CONCLUDED THAT A FOURTH LEG OF NEW GROWTH NOW MADE SENSE AND THAT THE MOST ATTRACTIVE PLACE TO LOOK WAS IN FOREIGN MARKETS.

## BACK TO THE OLD DRAWING BOARD

*Charles Darwin argued that all living things are constantly exploring and attempting to adapt to new habitats. For both finches and corporations, however, habitat expansion is a risky exercise, and there are countless examples of companies that pushed too far into foreign environments and lived to regret it. In order to stay vital and stretching to its full potential it was mandatory for The North West Company to expand, but some of those exploratory forays didn't pan out.*

*In 1993, North West struck a partnership with the largest retail chain in Greenland, KNI A/S. When the NWC catalogue was released in Greenland it was big news because North West was selling brand names like Levi and Nike at prices that undercut the Danish distributors already servicing the market. The excitement was short lived, however, when those same competitors whistled for their lawyers, who pointed out that the Danes owned the territorial rights to Greenland. Also, North West's partners struggled at translating the catalogue into Greenlandic (a form of Inuktitut) and Danish, and by the time the catalogues came out, two months of the selling season had already gone by. As a final straw, First Air suspended its regular flights to Greenland, which meant that North West no longer had a carrier to transport its goods across the north Atlantic. Two years after the promising partnership was formed, it was dead in the water.*

**143**

COMBINED WITH THE EXPERTISE IT HAD DEVELOPED SERVING SMALL, LOGISTICALLY CHALLENGING COMMUNITIES IN THE CANADIAN NORTH (AND THEN ALASKA) THE NORTH WEST COMPANY WAS EQUIPPED TO SUCCEED IN MARKETS THAT DETERRED OTHERS.

Russia. In 1994 the company hired a full-time Russian employee to organize business connections in eastern Russia, and Edward Kennedy and Earl Boon were preparing to fly to Yakutsk (the largest city in the far east republic of Sakha) when they learned that their Russian employee had just been murdered. Shortly afterwards, the Canadian Security and Intelligence Service contacted North West and informed the company executives that their late employee had close links to the former Soviet intelligence agency, the KGB — which is not all that unusual in Russian business circles.

Most retailers would look at remote communities in places like Russia, Greenland and the far-flung islands of the South Pacific and conclude that the complexity showed anything but potential. The South Pacific, for example, may look like paradise in tourist brochures, but it isn't necessarily idyllic for the stores that do business there or for the people who live there. Like stores in the north, many of the South Pacific's island nations have economic limitations, political challenges and more than their share of social issues. But to a patient and adaptable retailer like North West these market and social situations presented an opportunity to serve and help make a positive difference to local services and the quality of life overall. Combined with the expertise it had developed serving small, logistically challenging communities in the Canadian north (and then Alaska) The North West Company was equipped to succeed in markets that deterred others.

Rex Wilhelm was by now the President of North West's Alaska international division, and he began to play a key role in the Guam initiative. As the reader may recall, Rex grew up on a farm in Washinton State and went to Alaska in 1984. He began working at a rat-infested store in Nome. Over the years, he dealt with these and many other challenges, ranging from the awesome (blizzards and polar bears) to the mundane (frozen toilets.) At some point, it occurred to him that what hadn't defeated him had made him stronger, and he no longer wanted to leave Alaska. "It's hard to explain to outsiders," he says. "But when you're accustomed to difficulty, you actually begin to enjoy it. Our employees and store managers are special people — they actually prefer working in isolated, difficult conditions. Every day brings different challenges, and running a remote store gives them a sense of accomplishment. They'll tell you that they wouldn't want to work at a Sobeys or a Safeway. They'd find it too regimented and too predictable. They want to push themselves and build something that they can say is their mark, their legacy. They're adventurers by nature. And for me, that's pretty much the spirit of The North West Company. We excel at doing business in hard-to-reach markets. The circumstances that scare off other companies actually play to our strengths."

Kennedy refers to these disincentives as "entry barriers." "At first glance the South Pacific market appears completely different from what we do in North America, but looking closer,

FEBRUARY 11, 2012
NWC holds 25th Anniversary and Gala dinner for the 220 managers plus another 900 employees and guest Peter Mansbridge. Susan Aglukark performs, along with a steel drum band, First Nations drummers and dancers. One hundred seventy-one staff members are honoured for 25 to 52 years of service.

it's an exceptional strategic fit with our ability to serve physically and culturally distant markets. The islands have infrastructure challenges, somewhat unpredictable political conditions, extreme climates and elongated supply lines. They also have special staffing requirements, in the sense that successfully managing within these environments is a very rewarding role for a very select group of candidates with the right interests, values and skills. All these factors are deterrents for retailers geared to serve highly connected and developed urban markets."

North West's next step was similar to the initial scouting of Alaska Commercial in 1990 — they flew to Guam in 2006 to conduct reconnaissance. "I was incognito when I checked out Cost-U-Less stores, so I don't think they knew what was going on. We looked at how dense the retail marketplace was — at 150,000 people — compared to the amount of retail space and it was clear that there was room for more stores. K-Mart was at the time the only large American retailer in Guam, and while the company has been in decline for some time, their foreign division, K-Mart International, was, and continues to be, one of their most profitable operations."

The logistics of shipping to Guam were likewise attractive. Pacific islands may be worlds apart in terms of latitude, but there are important commonalities. The departure points for ships resupplying American territories in the South Pacific are Seattle and California, and Seattle is also the outbound hub for shipping to Alaska, Kennedy points out. "We thought it would be feasible to combine support services, including distribution and logistics, with our Alaska operations and gain lower costs through more volume. We also liked the fact that they were English speaking territories. From our experience in Alaska, we were gaining more knowledge of American consumer tastes and behaviour. We felt Guam was potentially another version of Alaska."

Veteran Alaska Commercial store managers Joe and Cathy Chaffee had worked for Cost-U-Less in American Samoa before joining Alaska Commercial, and they also believed it was a good idea. "Cost-U-Less was a well run company with a solid performance record," says Joe Chaffee. "And both companies — especially North West — are excellent at serving low-income indigenous communities. You'd be surprised at the similarities between the South Pacific and the north."

Jim Oborne says that the board recognized the strategic fit between north and south. "We saw common traits to both businesses. Most of the Cost-U-Less markets were remote, like ours. We reasoned that bigger buying power and shipping usage would lower our overall costs of service. The seller shareholders were having problems among themselves and this promised to keep the price reasonable. Ultimately, though, it boiled down to a feeling of confidence that we could succeed in the international marketplace. We wouldn't have had the balls to consider such a faraway acquisition if Edward, Rex, Jerry Bittner, Dick Hodge and the rest of the team hadn't done such a good job in Alaska."

## TO BUILD OR BUY?

In 2007, 10 years after he first opened his file on the South Pacific, Kennedy presented his findings to The North West Company board in Winnipeg. "Our pitch to the board was, let's build a store in Guam," he says. "We weren't interested in starting with an acquisition of Cost-U-Less because they also had stores in the Caribbean and we felt that was a stretch for us. So our plan was to 'green field,' which means to build from the ground up. The board approved our plan to study the feasibility of building a store but we couldn't start construction until we presented the costs to the board and they gave us the go-ahead."

Board member Jim Oborne says the fact that the board even considered the Cost-U-Less project was proof of how much confidence The North West Company had gained since it first went out on its own. "Alaska was not such a courageous leap because it was on the same latitude as northern Canada, had many of the same logistical issues and the communities were very similar. Giant Tiger was somewhat of a no-brainer too,

146

**2012**
Cost-U-Less Hilo celebrates 20 years of serving its community.

**2012**
Alaska Commercial Company recognized for partnership with Alaska School Activities Association.

because by launching Giant Tiger stores in Thompson, Prince Albert, The Pas and other centres across the mid-north, we were recapturing some of the business we were losing to out-shopping from smaller northern communities. And for a variety of reasons the Giant Tiger outlets in the cities of the south made sense for us too. But Cost-U-Less was a different matter. It was halfway around the world and, at first, it seemed to be a very different retail business."

After getting a provisional go-ahead from the board, Kennedy sent North West's team of construction experts to Guam to size up the cost of land and construction. "That's when we started to see challenges," says Kennedy. "It was an education for us, to be on the outside looking in for a change. One of our advantages is that we are well established in communities where new construction costs make it very expensive to start from scratch. The smaller the community, the more prohibitive the economics because you're splitting a market of a few thousand people with incumbent stores that have a lower cost base. So Guam began looking like a riskier proposition than we anticipated."

Another option was to reconsider acquiring an existing store chain like Cost-U-Less, but that was risky too. "For the sake of going into Guam with two Cost-U-Less stores, we'd be buying nine other stores, some of them in the Caribbean," explains Kennedy. "We're used to geographic breadth but we didn't have a feel for the Caribbean yet. So, we were getting concerned about whether this idea was as great as we thought."

## BETTER TO BUY

The Guam new store project was beginning to look more like a minefield than a viable growth path. Then, in May 2007, Cost-U-Less announced that it was going to "strategically review its business" — corporate-speak for saying that you are in trouble and open to offers. "I didn't think they were going to downsize,"Kennedy says, "because they only had 11 stores and couldn't get any smaller. They had a store under construction in

Grand Cayman and, as we found out, it was grossly over-budget and was stretching them financially. So we thought, okay, let's look at it again. They're not going anywhere. They're orphaned and too small to even be a public company. Some of the stores had strong sales but with their high overhead costs, the entire company was still only modestly profitable. We called them and asked them if they were for sale. And they said, 'We might be, and if we are, we'll put you on the list.'"

Kennedy and the North West team didn't want to give the impression of being too keen, but as they worked the numbers to set a value for Cost-U-Less versus building their own chain store-by-store, the purchase option emerged as much more attractive. "We looked at CUL's trading price, the square footage of the stores and the sales. It was going to cost us $300 a foot or more to build a single 40,000-square-foot store, and when we considered their established sales — at over $200 million a year — we felt that buying the company was the better choice."

In August 2007 The North West Company finalized the purchase of Cost-U-Less for $52 million. In the deal, the company acquired 12 stores — one in Fiji, one in American Samoa, two in Guam, one in California, two in Hawaii, two in the Netherland Antilles, two in the U.S. Virgin Islands and one under construction in the Cayman Islands. The CUL network was folded into a new division called The North West Company International with Alaska Commercial, under the leadership of Rex Wilhelm, and as Kennedy and everyone else on the team anticipated, the takeover wasn't without growing pains.

International economic woes soon put a crimp in tourism throughout the Caribbean, Hawaii and the South Pacific, which impacted CUL's sales base at the same time that high fuel prices drove up utility and transportation costs. Time zone differences, fuel cost inflation and regulatory details created their own challenges. "One of our stores is in Sonora, California," says Kennedy. "And on my desk will land a liquor license form that requires a criminal record check of the CEO. That regulation is unique to California,

147

2012
Eleven Northern communities lace up and hit the pavement to promote diabetes prevention in first annual North West Run for Diabetes event.

2012
NWC begins to freight products by air from its main Winnipeg distribution centre directly to Baffin Island. This initiative exceeds $600,000 and results in price reductions of 15 percent or more on 175 key products.

>>

OUR EMPLOYEES AND STORE MANAGERS ARE SPECIAL PEOPLE — THEY ACTUALLY PREFER WORKING IN ISOLATED, DIFFICULT CONDITIONS. EVERY DAY BRINGS DIFFERENT CHALLENGES, AND RUNNING A REMOTE STORE GIVES THEM A SENSE OF ACCOMPLISHMENT. THEY'RE ADVENTURERS BY NATURE. AND FOR ME, THAT'S PRETTY MUCH THE SPIRIT OF THE NORTH WEST COMPANY.

## IT'S ALL BEEN GREAT FUN!

*If you drive down the south coast of Newfoundland you eventually come to the small seaside community of Fortune, where Guy Strickland grew up. Like many young Newfoundlanders, Guy Strickland developed a tolerance for hardship and a taste for adventure. When he was a teenager, he lucked into a summer job at the Hudson's Bay store in Happy Valley. "I loved it so much I stayed on," he says. "I transferred to other locations, working my way up to store manager and then district manager and went all across the north. It was a really good time and I worked with Nor'Westers like Sidney Goodyear and Roy Emberley. Tremendous people, all of them."*

*Strickland was based in Winnipeg in 2007 when Edward announced that North West was buying a southern chain of stores called Cost-U-Less. "Well, that was a real surprise. Everyone was looking at each other like, what's going on? Then Edward explained it more, and we realized hey, it looks profitable, and it looks interesting. Instead of blizzards we'll have hurricanes."*

*Two years later, Strickland was given the opportunity to manage the new store on Grand Cayman. He says he was "very happy" with his life in Winnipeg and didn't want to move. "But my friends convinced me to look at the offer. So I flew down and checked it out, and oh yeah, it was nice. I went out for dinner with Tom Kalio, the Vice President of Cost-U-Less, and we connected right off the top. So I took the job, and I don't regret it for one second."*

*He says he calls the Grand Cayman store "the Taj Mahal" because it's such a beautiful building. "Everything is brand new. It's a great box. But there are challenges, of course. This is a very different environment, for one thing. And it's a real difference to go from temperatures of minus-30 for six months of the year to temperatures of plus-30 all year round. But like other Nor'Westers I'm used to different cultures, and though I'm a northern boy I'm not a big lover of winter, so it's all been great fun."*

*Strickland says he's noticed a lot of similarities between the people of Grand Cayman and the people of the north. "I hear it in the way people talk. With "Northern time" and "Island time" there's no rush, no sense of urgency. People here enjoy life. They're a lot like Newfoundlanders. Every day is another beautiful day."*

*Like a true northerner, he's made sure that the Cost-U-Less store looks after its neighbours. "One of my favourite charities is Meals on Wheels. They make meals and deliver them to elderly people or the less fortunate. We also help the Red Cross quite a bit, and we do some fundraising for the local chapter of the diabetes association. Last week we helped raise money for kids with special needs so they could go and swim with the dolphins. Oh yeah, that was a happy day. We were having a blast, every one of us."*

ABOVE: Guy Strickland (far right) and his Cayman Island team celebrate St. Patrick's Day.

## MAY FONG

*May Fong grew up in Fiji and moved to Europe to pursue a career in tourism and real estate management. She traveled the world, honed her poise and her skills in public relations, and in 1997, came back to her homeland with two daughters at her side. "Coming in from the airport I saw this large grey building with a Cost-U-Less sign. I thought, 'I wonder what sort of business is that?' Little did I realize I would be spending my next 15 years there!"*

*She started with Cost-U-Less that same year as a supervisor of checkout cashiers. "I encourage my cashiers to be themselves, and to be cheerful. If someone has been waiting too long in line, they might be cranky and aggressive. But if you give them a warm smile and say, 'thank you for your patience,' it changes the tone right away. I tell my cashiers, 'it's more work to frown than to smile, so make your day easier by smiling.'"*

*She lived through the coming and going of six store managers, and each time she was "given the keys to the store" and asked to act as interim manager until a new candidate was chosen. "I guess they thought I looked trustworthy," she laughs. After six managers, she says that she had "won the confidence" of her superiors, and they finally made her store manager in 2001. "I tell everyone who works for me — think big!" she says. "With the North West Company, there's no limit to how high you can go. Today, you might be bagging groceries, but look at me. If you work hard, you too can be a store manager one day."*

and is just a small example of the ongoing complexities of doing business in different jurisdictions, each with unique requirements. On the whole we've handled it very well. As a company we've become very good at dealing with complexity."

Kennedy acknowledges that "handling complexity well" doesn't sound all that exciting. But it is a key subplot of the company's success story. "To put it all together requires a massive team effort and adaptability without the benefit of a lower-cost, "one-size-fits-all approach" used by mega retailers serving larger markets," he says. "It takes the flexible expertise of our buyers, construction, our technology and accounting support, store development, loss prevention experts, human resources, administration, payroll, tax people and many others — all of them handling unique jurisdictional requirements, often one jurisdiction or currency per store, and across the international date line. We could be dealing with a First Nation chief and council in one store situation and the prime minister of an island nation in another."

"Making CUL work better has been a well-known challenge at North West. It was tricky and complicated to merge the computerized systems, personnel and corporate cultures. We put enormous effort into system integration," says Kennedy,

"And although that subject might put people to sleep, it's been a major, major point of pain and difficulty for other retailers. It gave us tremendous difficulty, but it didn't stop us. We persisted, remained true to our company values, and today, Cost-U-Less is fully integrated into The North West Company."

The Cost-U-Less acquisition and integration was also the completion of a long journey for The North West Company. It had traveled far and wide, established stores and distribution centres and transportation centres around the world, grown its revenues fivefold, achieved Derek Riley's vision of becoming a billion-dollar company and, most importantly, it had helped make shopping for everyday needs  healthier, more affordable and certainly more enjoyable for its thousands of customers.

>>

2012
Sixty-three staff members from the Northwest Territories, Nunavut, northern Alberta, Saskatchewan, Manitoba, Ontario, Nunavik, Alaska, Washington State and the Cayman Islands hit the ground running in the annual Cayman Islands Marathon in support of the Canadian Diabetes Association, American Diabetes Association and Cayman Islands Diabetes Association.

# A SHARED
# EXPERIENCE

## I LOVE IT BECAUSE IT'S BIG

*When I was young I moved from Rankin Inlet to the village of Arviat, to live with my grandmother. She was a hard worker and she was always singing. Every morning at 7:00 a.m. she went to church and then to her job at the health centre. My dad worked for the hamlet, driving the dump truck and the loader. When he wasn't working he would go out on the land, hunting and fishing. He would hunt seals in the spring, when the ice was breaking up, and caribou in the summertime. I used to love going with him, but I didn't like staying out overnight. Too many bugs and mice! My favourite thing was going fishing. My dad passed away eight years ago so now I go fishing with my husband. When I say "Let's go out!" he knows that I mean "Let's go fishing!"*

*The funny thing is, I'm allergic to fish! I can't eat it, so I give all my fish to the elders, and I shop for my food at the Northern store. I have eight children and eight grandchildren and I'm an auntie, so I have a lot of mouths to feed. I've had jobs at the elementary school as a teacher, a substitute teacher and a janitor, but my favourite job is taking care of my family because I love my kids. The Northern store is a great place to shop. I love it because it's big, like a Wal-Mart. There are so many different things on the shelves you feel like you're shopping in a city. They have good prices, too. There's always something on sale. And once a month they have the Family Allowance Giveaway, where they give you something free if you spend over $200.*

— ROSIE MAMGARK, NORTHERN CUSTOMER
IN ARVIAT, NUNAVUT

## THIS IS WHAT WE DO HERE

*I'm 42 years old, and I've worked for the Northern for 25 years. My pay stub says my retirement date is 2034, which is a long ways away yet! I work as a stock clerk, which means setting the goods out on the shelves and putting away freight.*

*My brother has been with the Northern for even longer than me — 34 years. He called me up one day 25 years ago and said I should be working here, so I started part time. I really liked it, so I moved on to full time and have been working there ever since. I've worked at many different jobs around the store, but my favourite is working the floor, because I like talking to the customers.*

*I also like helping out the new clerks. I tell them, "This is how we act, this is what we do here, don't be late," and all the rest. After all my years at the store I know what it takes to be a good employee and I help them do their best.*

— PHILLIP OTTUK, NORTHERN EMPLOYEE
IN ARVIAT, NUNAVUT

## TAKING TIME TO STOP AND CHAT

*I was born in Scotland, raised in London and have lived in Winnipeg since 1961. That puts me well over the retirement age, but I'm an artist — a sculptor — and artists never really retire. I'm a regular customer at the Giant Tiger in downtown Winnipeg. I live downtown so it's convenient for me to walk there, but I like Giant Tiger because it's a friendly store with great customer service.*

*I used to shop at the Eaton's department store but it closed several years ago. That's when I went in to have a look at Giant Tiger. They were sold out of a shirt that I wanted, and Mike the manager said he would call me when it came in. I didn't expect him to call but he did. My relationship with the store started from there.*

*The second manager, Kelly, always takes time to stop and chat with you. The other employees are very good too. The store has a wide selection of food and the clothes are good quality, so I'm very happy that Giant Tiger moved into our neighbourhood.*

— RODERICK SHIELS, GIANT TIGER CUSTOMER IN WINNIPEG

## GOOD SERVICE AND RESPECT

*I'm 67 years old and I've lived at Island Lake most of my life. I know Northern very well. As a matter of fact I worked at the local store myself one winter, back when it belonged to the Hudson's Bay Company. Nowadays I do all my shopping at the Northern store because it gives good service and it treats all its customers with respect. In return, I try to be a good customer and I always pay my bills on time.*

*Ian, the store manager, knows us well. He supports community activities and he often joins in himself. The store is on an island, so it's difficult to get to it right now when the ice is moving. The rest of the time you get a ride to the island by boat. The store has its own truck on the island and after you've done your grocery shopping, they will give you a ride back to the landing in their truck. The people really appreciate that. In the winter, you can drive across the ice, so the store manager will get the truck and drive the shoppers right to their house. When they give service like that it shows that they really appreciate their customers.*

— LUKE HARPER, NORTHERN CUSTOMER
IN ISLAND LAKE, MANITOBA

## THE GO-TO RETAILER

*I'm an Alaskan native, and I manage the store in Alaska with my husband. My dad worked for Alaska Commercial his whole life, so the company is in my blood. We've worked for Alaska Commercial in a number of communities around Alaska, and we've made lifelong friends in each place. It's a great job. Our customers are loyal to us, and we are loyal to our customers.*

*Ever since North West took over Alaska Commercial, the company has worked hard to become "the go-to" food retailer in the rural parts of the state. We consider our customers to be part of our family, and we know they feel the same way because they bring us fish, berries and other signs of their friendship. That's the best gift you can give, because it helps cut the isolation that comes with living in a remote area.*

—JESSIE CAMPBELL, ALASKA COMMERCIAL STORE
MANAGER IN KODIAK, ALASKA

## I BUY MY FAVOURITE FOODS THERE

*I live in the north end of Winnipeg. I've had a job for 20 years in the Reed bag factory and have also worked as a nanny. I know a bit about the food retailing business because my husband and I owned and operated a food store in this neighborhood for 20 years. The store was owned and operated by our own company, called Hyworon Enterprises. I still have my son, Walter. But my daughter died of cancer at the age of 52 and my husband has passed away. So here I am, 75 years old, and I have to watch my pennies!*

*I simply love Giant Tiger. Let me tell you, they not only have the best prices in town but also the best service! I buy my favourite foods there — chocolate milk, rye bread and bananas. I eat so many bananas that the store staff must think I am turning into a monkey. I have mobility problems because I was recently run over by a truck; the driver said he didn't see me! I've been struggling to recover, and the people at Giant Tiger have been very kind to me. I can't say enough nice things about them. They are quick and efficient and, to me, the cashiers are just angels.*

*— POLLY HYWORON, GIANT TIGER CUSTOMER IN WINNIPEG*

## A FRIENDLY PLACE

*My husband, Charles, and I are part-time musicians, playing mostly Latin and Cuban music. We have lived on the islands our whole lives, growing up in Honolulu and moving to Hilo in 1992. Charles works for another food store on the island, and I'm a foster care mom, with four permanent foster children and another emergency-care child — so we have five children in total.*

*I love CUL because we have so many kids and we can buy groceries there in bulk. The store also has more brand-name stuff and more variety compared to the others. We buy a lot of vegetables there, canned food like corn, and cereals that the kids like. It's a friendly place too — Mike, the manager, has gotten to know us and he says hi to the kids when we come in.*

*— JEANNIE BARGAS, (NATIVE HAWAIIAN) COST-U-LESS CUSTOMER IN HILO, HAWAII*

## FINDING EVERYTHING I NEED

*My name is Loretta "Rhett" Arch and I live in the Cayman Islands. I have come to love Cost-U-Less for many reasons. My husband and I entertain frequently for large groups and I love Cost-U-Less, just love it. I shop there because I'm able to find everything I need for my parties. Their meat department is excellent. The employees are very helpful, with personal touches that really impress me. I also do my general shopping there because their prices are so unbelievably discounted. If I see something I like at Cost-U-Less, I know I'd better buy it because it will sell out quickly.*

*I'm very busy with volunteer work, so another reason I shop at Cost-U-Less is because of their help in the local community. It's obvious that they take charity very seriously and have a passion for helping others. Because of their charitable spirit, I tell newcomers to the island to shop there and support them. The store manager, Guy Strickland, is just fantastic. He takes a special interest in his customers and makes an effort to know everyone by name. Guy is a giving person. I've heard that once a month he takes his entire staff out for dinner and sometimes a movie. He gets the store involved in so many charities that it spills over to the employees. It's a well-known fact that if you're having trouble getting support for a charitable project on the island, you just go and see the people at Cost-U-Less and your problem is solved.*

*— LORETTA ARCH, COST-U-LESS CUSTOMER IN CAYMAN ISLANDS*

## I WAS THE ONLY
## BALD FEMALE

I've lived in Attawapiskat all my life, and since I'm a single mother with three young daughters, I'm very thankful to have a job to support my kids. When I started working at the local Northern store I was a cashier, then I moved into the office, then I started working retail sales on the floor. Recently I got promoted and I work back in the office, so I've done most of the jobs in the store.

My favourite part is serving customers, talking to them and helping them in any way I can. The customers must know that I like helping them, because they always ask for me if they need something. They don't understand that I'm not working on the floor anymore, so they will come back in the office and ask about the bread or something, and I'll always help them even though it's not really my job.

I really appreciate the way the Northern store supports the people of Attawapiskat. One time we had a fundraiser for a woman who had breast cancer. We volunteered to shave our heads to raise money, and six people from the store did it, including me. I was the only bald female in the store, but it felt great! Doing things for people is the best part of my job.

—FLORENCE MATTHEWS, (CREE) NORTHERN
ADMINISTRATIVE MANAGER IN ATTAWAPISKAT, ONTARIO

## JUST JOKED ABOUT IT

I've been working at the Northern since 1994. I remember my first day of work. The manager told me to stock the dairy section with milk. I overfilled the cart so that it turned over and spilled milk all over the place. I was really scared of the manager at that time and I thought he would fire me. But he just joked about it. That made me more comfortable and soon it became one of those stories you can laugh at.

Now I love my job. I enjoy communicating with the customers as they come in to pick up their mail and packages. I also like to meet and talk to new people and have fun at work. When I started, I thought I'd always be a stock boy, but our manager really understands us and gives us new challenges. When the post office position came open I went after it, and now I'm working with money in an office setting. I know more about the post office than anyone in the store.

—THOMAS KOMAK, NORTHERN EMPLOYEE
IN ARVIAT, NUNAVUT

## A FAMILY TRADITION

My father was a store manager for the Hudson's Bay Company here in Rigolet before I was born, so the Northern Stores are a family tradition. I began my own career with The North West Company in 2000. I started work as a cashier, then moved on to being a grocery clerk along with freight duties. I believe The North West Company is truly interested in progressing my career, so I enjoy coming to work every day and learning new skills.

— KEITH FAULKNER, NORTHERN GROCERY CLERK
IN RIGOLET, LABRADOR

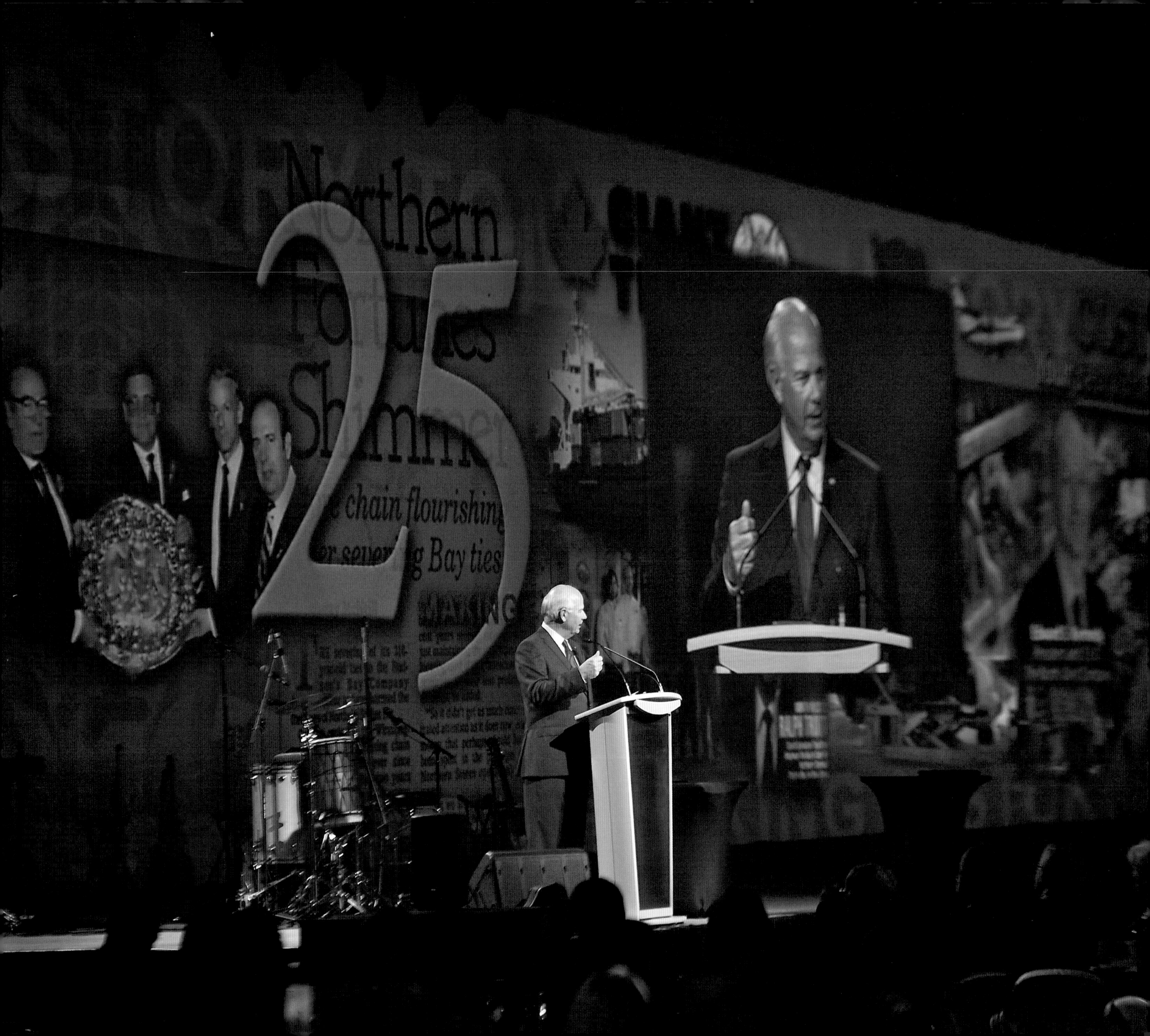
Northern
25
chain flourishing
Bay ties

# TRACING A REMARKABLE JOURNEY

WE'VE MOVED WITH THE ADVENTURING SPIRIT OF THE GREAT
NORTHWEST COMPANY EXPLORER, ALEXANDER MACKENZIE,
AND THE MANAGEMENT SKILLS OF OUR HUDSON'S BAY COMPANY
PREDECESSOR, GEORGE SIMPSON. COMBINED IN THE RIGHT
BALANCE, APPLIED TO THE RIGHT SITUATION, THEY ARE POWERFUL
INGREDIENTS BEHIND NORTH WEST'S LONGEVITY.

OPPOSITE: To celebrate The North West Company's 25th Anniversary in style, 220 managers from the Caribbean, South Pacific, Alaska and Northern and Western Canada converged in Winnipeg for training and a spectacular dinner and gala. The Company also invited 900 employees, retirees and friends. First Nations drummers and dancers and recording artist Susan Aglukark were among the night's performers, February 11, 2012. PREVIOUS: CBC's Peter Mansbridge was the Master of Ceremonies for the celebrations.

At The North West Company, "enterprise" and "enterprising" are special words. We've used them formally since 1990 when we secured our name and created our first logo, fondly referred to as the "bumble bee" and then replaced with our voyageur logo in 2006. Both designs celebrate our innovation, our spirit and our authentic link to the first great Canadian enterprise that began with the Hudson's Bay Company's early coalitions of Montreal fur merchants and their trading partners.

How does The North West Company endure, and with such robustness? The stories within this book give the answer. They trace a remarkable journey defined not by profit or size but by the collaboration of people, indigenous and newcomers, who live and work together to bring goods and services to some of the most remote regions of the world. Their daily work demands such skill, energy and adaptability that it serves as the very definition of the word "enterprise."

While these recollections accurately capture events and progress of the past 25 years, they reveal much more about the sustaining nature of who we are. Each personal experience seems to start as a commitment to nothing less than adventure. Then, inevitably, a deeper bond is forged — a bond that comes from living and serving others amidst challenging conditions and knowing that your work truly helps make our customers' lives better.

It would be a tempting, romantic description to say that today's North West Company continues to be an endeavour against great odds. Certainly, when assessed from start to end, our progress has gone beyond what seemed possible in 1987. (Although our first chairman, Derek Riley, did envision our future as a billion-dollar-plus company.) The greater truth is more methodical and disciplined. We in fact needed and used every year of the past 25 to move forward, and at times take a step back or sideways, by taking measured risks towards building a lasting business. It's been a steady march, not a cavalry charge. For periods we were outpaced and certainly out-headlined by larger retailers yet our cumulative results are ahead of most. This was no small feat. Recall that we started in 1987 as a private company with indebted investors and our task was no easier once we became publicly traded and subjected ourselves to the spotlight of daily stock valuations and quarterly results.

Staying vital and relevant are elements of our success that deserve mention. We have renewed our company countless times over decades of change and upheaval within the communities and countries that we serve. At the source is an ability to channel natural tensions between a never-ending desire to explore interesting new paths and the day-to-day accountability that we have to our customers, communities, investors and to each other. We've moved with the adventuring spirit of the great Northwest Company explorer, Alexander Mackenzie, and the management skills of our Hudson's Bay Company predecessor, George Simpson. Combined in the right balance, applied to the right situation, they are powerful ingredients behind North West's longevity.

## OUR CUSTOMERS AND COMMUNITIES

We are privileged to serve and work with wonderful people. They live in communities that are virtually right next door and getting virtually closer all the time, thanks to technology. Physically, our customers remain very distant — a few hundred or thousand

individuals living a few hundred or thousands of kilometres from the world's population centres. Contrasts can be seen in other ways, from the beauty, bounty and harshness of the land to the enduring cultural elements and the uprootedness of societies in transition.

Our customers remain incredibly diverse in their needs, despite having increasingly shared information and perspectives. Income differences persist as do the degree to which traditional lifestyle activities are preserved. At the same time our customers have access to an increasing range of products and services and expect more from us than ever before.

As their local store we welcome this. We see ourselves as agents working to bring the right range of products and services uniquely suited to each customer we serve. From a community perspective we accept their trust that we continue to be a committed local investor, employer, business partner and neighbour. Together it adds up to the type of complexity and reward that we embrace and that others shy away from.

AS LONG AS WE EMBRACE THE ESSENCE OF OUR ENTERPRISING SPIRIT AND KEEP DOING GREAT WORK ON BEHALF OF OUR CUSTOMERS IT WILL BE MORE THAN ENOUGH TO SUSTAIN US.

Looking forward, our markets are destined to assume more of the world's economic stage. In the north, warming climates and natural resources will shape the next era of relationships between indigenous people, nature and newcomers. At North West we are a bridge to the past and future. We have been part or have witnessed social and economic forces over three centuries and we have accumulated valuable wisdom and insight into what does and doesn't work. We have kept our distance when asked but we have readily stepped in to support community priorities whenever called upon. This respectful stance has stood the test of time and I believe it will be the basis for entirely new and mutually rewarding partnerships in the years ahead.

## THE PEOPLE OF
## THE NORTH WEST COMPANY

On a cold winter night this past February, 1,300 North West associates, retirees and friends of the company gathered at the Winnipeg Convention Centre to celebrate our 25th anniversary. The occasion also marked the first ever "Wintering Partners"

Conference of store managers from across our retail banners. While the week was a memorable introduction to snow and winter for our Cost-U-Less associates, the atmosphere inside at our gala evening had the familiar warmth of an island breeze. A highlight was the recognition of 55 active associates with 25 or more years' service who were in attendance plus another 118 that were at work in our stores. Three of these individuals, Gord Harkness, Camille Langlois and Don Coles, who the reader will recognize as one of our raconteurs, crossed the stage last to standing ovations in recognition of 50 years' service and counting. Sitting next to my table was our first Chairman, Derek Riley, and his nephew and our current Chairman, Sandy Riley — another symbol of the continuity and steadfast leadership throughout all levels of the Company.

As I watched the evening unfold, my thoughts slipped back to January 1990 — the second month of my career at North West. I had been invited to the Manitoba Club to celebrate, with others, the retirement of Clarence Mann, a long-serving Vice President. We sat around a large dining table and a piece of paper was

circulated on which each of us wrote our years of service. By the time it reached me there were a half dozen numbers, all in the 20s or 30s. I quickly and meekly scribbled the number 'two' with 'months' in parentheses and passed it on. The organizer of this exercise, who I recall was Earl Boon, then totaled the numbers and computed an average that, despite the dilution of Ralph Trott's and my brief tenures, still came out to over 25 years!

I recall often thinking in those early days that there was no way on this earth I would remain at any company for 5 years let alone 25 or more. Yet, at the same time, there was something genuine and truly accomplished about these experienced Bay men, now newly reminted as Nor'Westers. I speculated as to what impressions might be held by the many newer and younger Nor'Westers in attendance at the gala last February as they listened to and watched. Time will tell how many stay with us and for how long. I do know that as long as we embrace the essence of our enterprising spirit and keep doing great work on behalf of our customers it will be more than enough to sustain us.

*Edward Kennedy*

*President and CEO,*
*The North West Company*

At the anniversary gala, 171 staff were honoured for 25 to 52 years of tenure. The nearly 7,000 Nor'Westers that work in our stores make customer service their first priority, says CEO Edward Kennedy. OPPOSITE: Derek Riley, former President of the North West Company, and Sandy Riley, current Chair of the Board of Directors for the North West Company.

# INDEX

Page numbers in *italics* refer to image captions or timeline items.

## PHOTO CREDITS

Images in this book are part of the collections of The North West Company, Giant Tiger, Alaska Commercial Company, Cost-U-Less, and their employees (past and present), unless otherwise noted.

### Source Identifiers

HBCA: Hudson's Bay Company Archives,
         Archives of Manitoba
LAC: Library and Archives Canada
NGS: National Geographic Society
ROM: Royal Ontario Museum

### Prologue

6: HBC Historical Collection, Manitoba Museum. Reproduction courtesy: HBCA, 1987/363-I-302/5 (N8198) *The Pioneers' Highway*. Oil painting by John Innes. 7: Hats, HBCA, 1987/363-C-308/2 (N8318) "Modifications of the Beaver Hat." From *Castorologia or the History and Traditions of the Canadian Beaver* by Horace T. Martin, 1892. Nonsuch, HBCA, 1987/363-N-18/51 (N7558). Design of general arrangement of the *Nonsuch* replica built by the Hudson's Bay Company. Drawn by Peter M. Wood. 8: HBCA, 1987/363-N-18/55 (N16440) "A chart to show the Voyage of the Nonsuch, Capt. Zachariah Gillam, 1668–1669." Drawing by Captain Adrian Small, undated (ca.1969). 9: Natasha Lakoš/ Echo Memoirs. 11: HBCA, 1987/363-N-18/47 (N53-A-184) "Camp of James Bay Indians at Charles Fort, 1668, with the *Nonsuch* anchored off shore." From the mural by A. Scheriff Scott in the elevator lobby of HBC Winnipeg store." 12: HBCA, 1987/363-H-22/5 (N16879) Postcard of North West Company plaque at Sault Ste Marie. 13: HBCA, 1992/10/1 (N16878) Retirement party for Currie McArthur at the Beaver Club, Queen Elizabeth Hotel, Montreal, October 12, 1960. 14-15: Natasha Lakoš/Echo Memoirs. 16: Alexander Mackenzie, LAC, Acc. No. R9266-3034. Peter Winkworth Collection of Canadiana. 17: Kevin Fleming/*National Geographic* Magazine, August 1987. 18: ROM, 979.64.1: "Canoe launching at Fort William, Ontario" (watercolour, pen and ink over graphite on woven paper), 1865–1905; Armstrong, William; ROM2006-7487-1: With permission of the Royal Ontario Museum © ROM. 21: HBCA, 1987/363-F-67/53 (N61-57) Illustration of Fort William in 1863. 22: Portrait, HBCA, P-167 (N5353) (T7887) "Mr. Samuel Hearne, Late Chief at Prince of Wale's Fort, Hudson's Bay" (Churchill). Engraving, coloured, 1796. Token, HBCA, "The North West Company's Beaver Token." From *Castorologia or the History and Traditions of the Canadian Beaver* by Horace T. Martin, 1892. 23: Natasha Lakoš/Echo Memoirs.

### Chapter 1

28: HBCA, *Moccasin Telegraph*, December 1942, p.8. 31: *Winnipeg Free Press,* Jeff DeBooy, August 17, 1989, reprinted with permission. 32: HBCA, *Moccasin Telegraph*, Summer 1987, p. 32. 38: Courtesy of Jim Oborne.

### Chapter 2

44-45: Courtesy of Don Coles. 49: Kevin Fleming/ *National Geographic* Magazine, August 1987. 54: HBCA, 1990/8/7 (N16875) "Unveiling of the new North West Company flag at press conference to launch 'The North West Company, Inc.' name [at] the Forks, Winnipeg, Manitoba, on March 16, 1990." 61: *Winnipeg Free Press,* Wendell Phillips, January 6, 1989, reprinted with permission.

### Chapter 3

65: Courtesy of Rex Wilhelm. 67: Courtesy of Rex Wilhelm. 71: Courtesy of Mark Melton. 85: Courtesy of Don Coles.

### Chapter 4

104: Getty Images. 122: Courtesy of Jim Deyell. 124: Courtesy of Bibianna King.

# ECHO MEMOIRS™

THIS BOOK WAS WRITTEN, DESIGNED AND PRODUCED BY

Echo Memoirs Ltd.
1616 West 3rd Avenue
Vancouver, BC
Canada V6J 1K2

WWW.ECHOMEMOIRS.COM
1 877 777 ECHO

*Creating distinctive company history and personal biography books since 1999.*

# ACKNOWLEDGEMENTS

*Charles Foran created a condensed version of our history leading up to 1987. He has woven a terrific story that helps the reader understand our legacy while stimulating us to learn more about the people of the fur trade and the early commercial development of Alaska and North West Canada.*

*Our primary author, Jake MacDonald, worked with extraordinary patience and Nor'Wester-like dexterity to paint an excellent literary picture of an incredibly multifaceted business history. Jake conducted over 50 interviews with Nor'Westers as part of his research and included dozens of personal interviews in this book. Thank-you to these participants for graciously sharing their time and thoughts. I hope all Nor'Westers, past, present and future, will see some part of their experience reflected in the recollections. These stories are about you and the incredible unbroken link between the first frontier merchants and today's North West Company.*

*Thank-you to all the Nor'Wester associates who tirelessly supported this project starting with David Lui, Jennifer Ching and the Marketing team. This was a lengthy task and definitely outside of your day-to-day roles.*

*Finally, my deepest gratitude to our nearly 7,000 fellow Nor'Westers who put their talents to work every day in our stores. You are the heart of our history. There would be no story without you. Great work, everyone!*

*President and CEO,*
*The North West Company*